SPL

SPLASH!
SWIMMING WITH WILKIE

David Wilkie
and Kelvin Juba

Photos by Miles Spackman

Based on the Channel Four
Television series

Stanley Paul
London Melbourne Sydney Auckland Johannesburg
in association with Channel Four Television Company Limited

Stanley Paul & Co. Ltd

An imprint of the Hutchinson Publishing Group

17–21 Conway Street, London W1P 6JD

Hutchinson Group (Australia) Pty Ltd
30–32 Cremorne Street, Richmond South, Victoria
3121
PO Box 151, Broadway, New South Wales 2007

Hutchinson Group (NZ) Ltd
32–34 View Road, PO Box 40–086, Glenfield,
Auckland 10

Hutchinson Group (SA) Pty Ltd
PO Box 337, Bergvlei 2012, South Africa

First published 1982
Text © David Wilkie and Kelvin Juba 1982
Photos © Stanley Paul & Co. Ltd 1982

Set in Linotron Univers

Printed in Great Britain by The Anchor Press Ltd
and bound by Wm Brendon & Son Ltd,
both of Tiptree, Essex

British Library Cataloguing in Publication Data
Wilkie, David
   Splash!
   1. Swimming
   I. Title   II. Juba, Kelvin
   797.2'1   GV837

ISBN 0 09 150280 2 (cased)
        0 09 150281 1 (paper)

To Olive

Acknowledgements

The author would like to acknowledge the work carried out by
the following: Channel Four Television, Dr D. Hunt, Sara Green,
Mrs Bernice Wilkins for providing overall advice, Barnet
Copthall and Hatfield Swimming Pool for photographic facilities,
and to Mike Mansfield for all his assistance as director of the
television series.

Contents

Foreword

I leant back against the yellow touch pads and could still feel the slight numbing at the back of my arms and the top of my legs. The feeling quickly passed, for as I lifted my goggles my mid-race feelings were confirmed by the clock on the wall. A world record by over 3 seconds – 2 minutes 15.11 seconds.

My life's ambition was achieved – a world record and an Olympic gold medal in one swim. I had spent the years since Munich competing and training for that one medal, and in that time had learnt a great deal about myself and my swimming. But, for all my dedication, other aspects of swimming had not passed me by. I still had a good understanding of the sport.

That understanding was now about to be carried into other fields. My gold medal and subsequent retirement closed one door but, as often happens in such cases, another door opened. My life suddenly branched into many more aquatic fields. Heavy demands were made on my time by television, writing, personal appearances and the like. Not all of them were involved with swimming. In some people's eyes, reaching the peak in one field automatically makes you an expert in many more, and I was called upon to give comments on topics of which I knew little.

However, swimming remains my first love, and in the six years since that Olympic gold, I have been able to add teaching and coaching experience to my knowledge as a swimmer. Together, I hope they make a book of interest, which will mean something to the non-swimmer and yet help the improver on his or her path to better swimming.

The most important factor that will emerge is that *anyone can swim*, and everybody should try. Like anything else, swimming, when you cannot do it, looks hard. When the initial fear has been overcome, swimming rapidly becomes easy. I hope that, having read this book and having seen the associated television series, you will be able to start yourself off.

My earlier book, *Winning with Wilkie*, was written with my competitive experience behind me and, in keeping with this, was essentially about competitive swimming. *Splash* is about the improver, and is based not just on my racing knowledge but also on the experience of the many people I have coached and taught in recent years.

1 Why Swim?

Swimming for Safety

According to recently released Home Office figures, in 1980 809 drownings were reported to the police. These probably make up only 75 per cent of all drownings in England and Wales. Most interestingly, nearly 40 per cent of the cases reported occurred in water of less than 1½ metres deep. A large proportion of victims were aged between twenty-five and seventy-five.

It is therefore true to say that many of our drownings occur in water in which people are not even required to swim. Common sense is often the hall-mark of survival in and around water. Swimming- and water-consciousness can be of great help there. Britain has certainly become a lot more aware since the Amateur Swimming Association's campaign 'Every Boy and Girl A Swimmer'.

The report also noted that over half of all rescues were made by members of the general public – the rest being made by members of the rescue services. In order to keep up this record of public rescues, it is vital that as many people as possible be competent swimmers. Again, swimming- and water-consciousness is the cornerstone of this success.

Before the Second World War, the number of drownings was even greater, though there were fewer swimming pools and less opportunity for people to swim. In those days, the swimming teacher was a rarity. Now, practically every town of more than 10,000 people has its own pool with instructors. More swimming pools mean more exposure to water and even more danger than before, especially to the young child – hence the figures on drownings in shallow water, though only 4 per cent of accidents occur in swimming pools.

And yet people have been aware of swimming for many centuries. There were eight public and 150 private baths in Constantinople in 430 AD, and 27,000 baths in Baghdad. Britain has been aware of swimming since the influence of the Romans on our bathing habits.

Fortunately, to counterbalance the dangers there has been greater attention to all aspects of swimming and to personal survival techniques. Some 310,000 awards were made during 1981 by the Amateur Swimming Association. Life-saving methods have also been improved and more people are now capable of drownproofing techniques.

Government spending cuts in recent years, however, have not helped. There is less opportunity to learn to swim at school than five years ago because of the economic situation. This has given all swimming authorities cause for growing concern. With these cuts it becomes even more important for parents to have the ability to swim and pass on their knowledge to their children. Too often we expect local authorities to assume responsibility and with more recreation spending cuts on the way, it is good to see parents taking a hand in teaching their children.

Swimming for Fun

Swimming has numerous advantages as a pleasure sport. In the first place, it has no off season: you can swim at any time of the year. It is also inexpensive. A swimming costume, goggles, float and armbands are the maximum amount of equipment generally required. None are costly and entrance to pools can be as little as 20p or 30p. In one town it is free, as a facility to the ratepayer.

Swimming can be great fun. These children are swimming a full range of strokes during the Channel 4 series 'Splash', which was filmed at the Barnet Copthall pool

When you actually start to move through the water, the feeling of propulsion, as well as the sensation of power as you glide or dive, can be a thrill. There are also lots of games that you can play in the water. And swimming competently opens up a wide field of other sports such as snorkelling, water skiing, sub-aqua, sailing and wind-surfing.

Swimming for Health

Swimming is often considered to be one of the healthiest sports. Recommended by many doctors, it is seen as the panacea for a range of ailments. It has the great advantage of not requiring the participant to support his or her body weight. Swimming is, therefore, of unique help to handicapped people, giving them the opportunity to exercise bodies that might otherwise be immobile. Blind and deaf people can swim. People with broken or damaged limbs can use swimming as a means of rehabilitating their muscles.

Yasuhiro Akumatsu is a fifty-six-year-old Japanese who suffered from radiation sickness after the 1945 atomic bombing of Hiroshima. He started swimming in 1975, after doctors had told him that there was no medical cure for his dangerously low white blood cell count. Now six years later, after swimming nearly 2000 miles, he has recovered.

Many outstanding swimmers have been asthmatics: one of the greatest is the American freestyler Rick Demont. After winning the 1972 Olympic title in the 400 metres, he was disqualified for using an asthma preparation that was considered illegal by the Olympic authorities. This enormous setback did not curtail Rick's love of the sport. Now twenty-six years old, he still competes for the USA over 100 metres and trains for one hour a day. Swimming, of course, can improve breathing and doctors prescribe it for respiratory defects.

Natural spas in Bath, Buxton and Harrogate were regarded as remedial bathing towns rather than holiday resorts during the 1700s. Britain's spas became popular for health reasons, despite our climate, as the homely equivalent of the continental spa. That swimming should be seen as such a healthy sport is ironic, since the water itself is a ready medium for transmitting all types of diseases and germs. The warm environment seems to provide a breeding ground.

Before starting out, please follow these simple rules:

1. never swim with a cold
2. use the footbath and the toilets before you swim
3. check with your doctor before swimming if you have an ear or eye infection or athlete's foot
4. take advice before swimming if you have a verruca.

2 The Magic of Learning

Water Babies

Very young babies move their limbs in water quite naturally. To be fully relaxed when holding a baby, it is very helpful if a mother and father are able to swim themselves and have complete confidence in the water. Feelings in such situations are very quickly transmitted.

Please remember, although babies can move their limbs naturally and keep themselves on the surface, they lack sufficient strength to actually swim. If a six-month-old fell in a river, the likelihood of its saving itself would be remote despite natural water instincts. These early stages are merely a matter of acquainting the child with the water, and even then it is highly unlikely that a baby remembers this early experience.

My advice to parents with a young baby is this: the earlier you start to get your child used to water, the better. Start in the bath at home. Fill the bath up as much as possible. Then get into the bath yourself, holding your baby carefully. Support baby from behind whilst sitting or lying on your back. Hold the child by putting your hands under its armpits, allowing your thumbs to act as a balancing mechanism at the back. Let it kick its legs and submerge underwater if necessary. Up to nine months of age, the breathing adaption will come quite naturally. Provided the child's face is not submerged for long periods, water will not be inhaled.

Bath toys can be a great help here as an enjoyment and distraction – so please use them. The great advantage of bathtime games is that they take place in a warm and familiar environment. You are away from the rather scaring splash and noise of a swimming pool.

By the time a baby is nine months old, the natural thrashing movements have ceased and children tend to lie rather rigid in the water. This may be a problem, but the important thing is to keep your child attending the pool regularly.

When you go swimming with your baby, start by blowing bubbles yourself. Young children learn by imitating. You may find that they will dribble the water out because they have tried to drink it. Eventually, they will learn to blow out, particularly if you make a noise with the bubbles. Then, blow on your baby's face to associate this with going under the water. The idea here is that when you blow hard, this makes the child close its eyes and hold its breath. The sequence of movements should be to lift, then lower, then blow, then go under. This slowly develops into a bobbing game.

Once the baby is happy going under the water, both parents working together are now ready to 'torpedo' baby over a short distance between them. This is achieved by one adult letting go of the child, who will automatically try to walk in the water towards the other. The adults should not be more than an arm's length apart. These movements can be slowly built up over a period of time, probably until your baby is about sixteen months old. The need for regularity cannot be overstressed and it is important that the swim sessions be happy. Nothing is ever achieved if the baby is forced, too cold, or very unhappy.

Acclimatizing the baby to the swimming pool can be important here. The transition from bath to pool has to be handled carefully. The practice of holding baby behind the head so as to allow it to lie on its back in the bath water can be transferred to the swimming pool. The feel of this position can help a baby get used to having its ears under the water, where the muffled sounds may at first be frightening. Again, practice at home can help.

In order that baby can experiment a little on its front in the bath tub, knot a number of handkerchiefs together and then loop them under baby's chin to keep its head clear of the water. A second loop of handkerchiefs under the child's stomach will help to get the correct body position.

Doctors recommend that young children under the age of six months should not swim until they have had all of the standard inoculations. It can be dangerous to do otherwise. On the other hand, to start in the bathtub at home from the third week after birth will improve all aspects of a baby's development.

Parents and Young Children

A very young child who is nervous is going to need every encouragement, even for the smallest achievement. Parents should try continuously to praise their child's progress, however small. Getting the face in the water comes easily to a small child at first. One of the problems in the first three years is actually getting the head *out* of the water. From that age on, the reverse problem may set in. If the child is nervous of getting his or her face in the water, start by wetting the face; slowly build this up until splashing water on the face becomes en-

Having fun in the water is what swimming is all about, as this typical mother and baby scene shows

joyable. Once this is achieved, you can then encourage the child to put his or her face down into the water.

As a very broad rule, a child will be three and a half years old before it has sufficient strength to swim with its head up. Many children can swim on their backs for quite long distances or dog-paddle with their heads down. The difficulty then is in taking a breath, where they may need parental help from the side.

Throughout the first three years there are several important procedures to remember. Try to take your child during a lunch hour or a non-busy time at the pool and do not leave him or her standing around too long in a draughty spot or walk the child through a cold footbath. Let the youngster get into the water gradually, and try to use shallow water at the end of a learners' pool if there is one. Goggles can be dangerous at a young age and should not be used. On the other hand, floats and armbands are acceptable, though the child should not become too dependent on armbands and should get used to the feeling of water pressure at least once in every session. So take the bands off from time to time.

3 A New Approach to Learning

Fear is the key for most people. If you have not learnt to swim by the age of five, this fear will multiply as each year goes by. Achieving that 'at home' feeling in water may take a considerable time. This will vary from person to person, as we are all individuals. I am going to suggest a slightly different learning approach to overcome this fear.

Try to select a quiet time at the pool. Get into the water carefully by climbing down the steps at the shallow end. Go in and lower your shoulders down to the level of the water. Now bend your knees and try to move them towards your chest. Put your feet back down. Now lift them again and try to feel the pressure of the water lifting your body slightly. Do this continually and try to move forward as you do it. Now lift your knees, keep your body vertical and try to keep the knees up for longer. Circle your hands in figure-of-eight movements by your hips to keep your body balanced.

Go to even shallower water. Kneel on the bottom and again just lift your knees. Try this once or twice. When you are confident, follow this by taking hold of two floats. You may feel tense at this point because you are about to put your body in a slightly unbalanced position, so remember to breathe naturally.

Wrap your hands over the top of each float. Kneel on the bottom and again just lift your knees. Try this a few times and when you feel confident, stretch your toes backwards so as to straighten your legs behind you. Now take hold of one float. Hold the sides of the float with your thumb up and try the same movement, but this time push the float out in front of you. Hold it out in front with your arms straight and keep moving across the pool.

Overcoming the First Fear

If you have a fear of water – and many people have this passed on to them, particularly if their parents never learnt to swim or showed little interest – it is important that you take your time in overcoming it. Fear of water is frequently transmitted within a family.

If you do feel tense, then just go down to the pool and splash about near the edge or in a shallow part of the pool. Try to use this as a means of getting to know the capacity of your own body and please, please take your time. One positive approach is to join a class at your local swimming pool for the very nervous. A reasonable number of pools have such classes.

Fun for Young Children

The introduction of groups of young children to the water should be fun. Often this can be achieved by playing team and partner games that they might play in the school playground. By using such games, fear is more quickly overcome. Tag, relays and What's the Time, Mr Wolf?, are great favourites, together with obstacle races, bubble-blowing relays, ball retrieval, or Simon Says: Bubble-blowing relays are best played with two or three teams of four learners or improvers. As the participants are young, the relay should not go on too long and become boring. The relay can only be carried out in water in which a youngster can stand or walk.

The first person on each team starts on 'go'. They walk or run to the other side of the learners' pool and have to lower their faces and blow on the surface of the water at least once

Swimming is one of the cheapest of all family sports

in every two paces. On touching the wall on the other side, the next person in the relay can leave the side and follow the same pattern. The winners would be the first team to complete the final leg of the relay.

Simon Says is great fun for very young children. The game has a leader who calls out, 'Simon says' followed by a command. The rest of the group obey the commands. The object is for the leader to catch members of the group out carrying out a command that has not been prefixed by the words 'Simon Says'. The leader in this case could be a parent or swimming teacher in the water and the ultimate aim is obviously to get the youngsters doing a great number of things in the water.

For example, the leader might start with, 'Simon says put your hands on your hips', and everyone must follow. The game can then be taken stage by stage to lead up to 'Simon says put your face in the water!' Obviously, in the early stages the leader doesn't want to catch too many people out because having half the group sitting on the side early on would mean fewer children trying new things.

What's the Time, Mr Shark? is the aquatic version of the playground game What's the Time, Mr Wolf? It is again played by a group in the learners' pool with a leader – known as The Shark. The Shark has his back turned and hands covered over his eyes as the group creep up on him.

One of the group then shouts, 'What's the time, Mr Shark?' The Shark then uncovers his eyes and shouts a time, for instance, 'Three o'clock!' As soon as he turns, the group must

stop moving towards him. Anyone he sees moving is considered out of the game and must sit on the side. Mr Shark then turns his back again and the group swim or walk in once more, getting closer to him. This pattern continues until some of the group get really close to him. On the final occasion, Mr Shark turns and instead of shouting a time and trying to spot moving people, he shouts 'Dinner Time' and tries to swim after and catch one of the nearest people. The victim caught becomes Mr Shark for the next game.

An Adult Approach

Many adults are even more afraid of putting their faces in the water than children. This fear tends to arise due to prior concern over breathing. Breaststroke is excellent to begin with as an adult, partly because of the breathing adaptation involved and partly because as we get older our ankles get stiffer. The type of stiff-ankled kick employed in breaststroke is normally easier for adults. Please remember, it *is* possible to swim without putting your face in the water.

Equipment in the Early Stages

The young swimmer seen here wearing arm bands and flippers and holding a float has all the equipment for the first stages. It is better to start without goggles even if the water does sting your eyes. The time may come when you land unexpectedly in the water and have to swim without goggles on. So do not become too reliant on them.

4 Front Crawl

Front crawl is the most efficient of the competitive strokes simply because it is the nearest of the four to continuous propulsion. It is therefore also the fastest. The first man to break 5 miles an hour was swimming front crawl. John Trembley recorded this speed some eight years ago at Long Beach, California, in a 50 yard race – some speed! Many of the less athletic among us would have difficulty in running at that pace.

It would be true to say that most men like to be seen swimming front crawl. It is very much a virile stroke. Mastering the appropriate breathing pattern is difficult and tends to put many women and children off.

The standard type of front crawl that one sees in public pools is one with head up and with breathing from side to side. What a waste of energy, and yet the average schoolchild tends to do it simply because the correct breathing has not been mastered. This frequently comes about because the technique takes time to explain and needs individual attention, whilst the large classes that attend school swimming lessons make it difficult to create time for this. So, whether you are a beginner or an improver, I would always recommend that you consult your local swimming-pool staff about joining their after-school or after-work classes, which are normally much smaller.

Starting

Assuming that you can float and kick your legs, the next stage on your front would be the dog paddle. Our animal friends tend to do this quite naturally and, with few exceptions, this is a relatively easy stroke for us as well.

Start from the front gliding position. Kneel in the water and then take your knees off the bottom, extending your legs back by simply pointing your toes and letting your feet float upwards towards the surface behind you. The arms should be outstretched in front and about shoulder-width apart at your fingers.

Try to kick your legs, propel yourself and yet keep your balance without going straight underneath the water. You might need to put your face under to achieve this, so follow the bubble-blowing routine mentioned in Chapter 3.

As soon as you go forward by kicking in this manner, you are ready to go into dog paddle. From the outstretched position, start to pull back towards your stomach with one hand and then, as soon as that hand gets in line with your stomach, start the pull with your other hand. The fingers on your hand should point to the bottom of the pool at the start of the pull. The hand is then cupped with the thumb uppermost and the arms angled in order that the pull can be made down an imaginary centre line running from head to foot under your body. Make the strokes long and bold. After the pull try to straighten your arms out in front of you in order to gain more distance per stroke, thereby using less energy to cover the distance travelled. When you have managed to control this and feel you have sufficient balance, try pulling back right *past* your stomach towards your thighs, each time keeping your thumb close to your hip.

Arm Action

You should now be ready to go on to the front crawl itself. Follow the same pulling mode as in the dog paddle, then simply lift your arm out of the water at the end of each pull. The arm is lifted over the water by bending your elbow at the end of the pull. Keep your thumb up against the side of your body as you lift your arm over the water – the elbow is held high during this recovery phase. Now drive your fingers slowly into the water approximately 30 centimetres in front of your head and shoulder.

The arm is then straightened at the elbow, and the rest of your arm follows into the hole made in the water by your hand. Once your arm has been fully extended onto an imaginary centre line beneath you (running down the middle of your body from head to foot), you are ready to start pulling your arm under your body and pushing back to your hips. Your fingers by the middle of the pull no longer face down, but sideways. Try to get the feeling of pulling your body over your hands.

Meanwhile, rather like the pedals on a bike, the opposite arm has started its recovery movement over the water and as the first arm fin-ishes its pull, the other should be entering the water at the opposite point.

It is best to get the feel of front crawl by doing all this with your face down on the water, keeping your head steady, until you run out of breath. Then just stand on the bottom and when you have recovered your breath, start swimming again. You can then open your eyes and make sure that your arms are in the correct position under your body. Do not worry about the breathing technique until you have really mastered this stage of mobility.

Correct Breathing

The key to breathing on all strokes, and on the front crawl in particular, is to be able to balance the pressure of the water with the air in your nose – you have to make a positive attempt to blow out through the mouth – normally something we don't need to think about on dry land. Unfortunately this adaptation can only come about through practice in the water. You may try it and the water will run into your nose and mouth and even your eyes, but through practice it will gradually get better.

a

d

Here you see my right arm entering first. Note that I breathe to the left and that I fully extend my left arm before beginning my pull. During the pull I keep my left elbow higher than my hand. My hands are very nearly at opposite points throughout the arm cycle

Stand in shallow water and bend forward. Now go through the arm movements you have been making in the water. Decide whether it would be better to breathe to the left or right side as a matter of personal comfort. This can be achieved by simply putting your face on the water and feeling which way you naturally want to turn. Then, starting with your face down on the water and eyes looking directly ahead, move your arms. If you feel more comfortable turning your head to the right, do so when your left hand enters the water and vice versa. Take a small, controlled breath and whilst turning your head, move your mouth back towards your shoulder. Open your mouth so that air can enter. In the water a bow wave, similar to that of a boat, forms in front of your head, with an air pocket immediately behind. Because of the protection of the bow wave and the subsequent air pocket, your head does not need to turn that much. The more you turn it, the more difficult it is to swim the stroke because the body line is destroyed.

If you find the timing of your breathing difficult, practise this movement on the poolside. Alternatively, practise in front of a mirror at home in order to observe what you are doing.

From the shoulder position you can now start to return your head to the front position ready to blow out through your mouth and nose. Your right hand now makes its recovery over the water and follows your head back to the central position. When your head faces the front you start to blow out through your mouth. Make no effort to blow out through your nose – this will happen automatically when air is expelled from the mouth. And so the cycle continues in time with the windmilling action of the arms. Those people who breathe to the other side should follow exactly the opposite pattern.

Now try the whole movement in a swimming situation. If when you try to swim and breathe you find that you are still not happy, come out onto the side and try it in slow motion again. Then return to the water and continue to practise until you have conquered the feel and rhythm of the movement.

Overcoming the Breathing Problem

The almost endemic early breathing problem relates to the position of the head at its return to the water. The breath has been taken to the side. Start to breathe out before the mouth makes contact with the water again. In other words, when you exhale, start by blowing out into the air before the mouth goes back into the water. Many learners imagine that they are breathing out at the right time, yet water enters the nose because they leave it too late. They return their faces to the water and think, 'I must blow out', and in the fraction of a second it takes for that thought to be transmitted and translated into action, water shoots up their noses.

Early exhalation can be the greatest single cure of breathing problems.

Leg Action

We have talked fairly thoroughly about your arms and breathing but not about your legs. Let your arms dominate the stroke in terms of rhythm and fit the legs in with it. Some swimmers may want to swim with six leg kicks to every arm cycle, particularly if they are going for speed (though this can be tiring), or you may try two or four kicks over a distance if you have strong arms and weak legs. The leg action stabilizes the body.

The leg movement for the front crawl is an alternating kicking action emanating from the hips. Try to keep your legs as straight as possible when kicking. They will naturally bend because of the water pressure on the upward kick, but it is best to think 'straight' as too much bend will allow your feet to come out of the water. Your heels should only just break the surface at the end of the upward kick. The depth of the downward kick should be 30 centimetres. It can help here if you try to keep your kick in line with your body depth in order to stay streamlined. Your ankles should be flexible and if you can keep them stretched this will give you a more effective kick. The leg motion should be aimed at trying to shake your feet off on the downward movement.

Try to let your legs kick as close together as possible. If you find it difficult to feel how close together your legs are, aim at letting the inside of your ankles brush each other as your legs kick up and down.

This sequence shows not only the correct position of the head, hands and arms but also the movement of the legs. My right hand enters the water as the left foot reaches its deepest point in the water, and vice versa. The relationship between the arms and legs produces the necessary balance for the whole stroke

Head and Body Alignment

With a heavy six-beat kick, your head needs to be carried high in the water for speed, your eyebrows resting on the water surface, and you need to be looking some 10 metres in front of you, along the bottom. Lifting your head by using your neck can place strain on your breathing and this higher head position can be achieved more satisfactorily by very lightly arching your back.

If you just want to keep fit and swim a certain number of lengths, your head should be lower and the kick less driving. In this case the hairline rests on the surface. This helps to relax your neck and your breathing. Most important of all, please remember to keep your head steady, as this will keep the body in the correct position. The body position should be flat and parallel to the surface of the water. Obviously this will deviate slightly with the movement of breathing.

Six *Splash* Checkpoints for Front Crawl

1. *Fault: My legs drop down too easily.*
   Correction: After breathing, when your head returns to the front, look directly down.

2. *Fault: My legs seem to tire after a short distance.*
   Correction: Make sure that you exhale all used air after you put your face back into the water.

3. *Fault: My arms seem to go too high during recovery.*
   Correction: Try to get your fingertips to scrape along the surface on the over-water movement.

4. *Fault: I can't feel whether my elbows are sufficiently high.*
   Correction: Try to show more and more of your armpits as your arms recover.

5. *Fault: I can swim front crawl but I get breathless after only a short distance.*
   Correction: Build up day by day, swimming a regular system of single widths at an easy pace with an even rest. Day by day increase the distance and hold the pace.

6. *Fault: My elbows seem to collapse when my hands enter the water.*
   Correction: Aim to pull with your forearm as well as your hand.

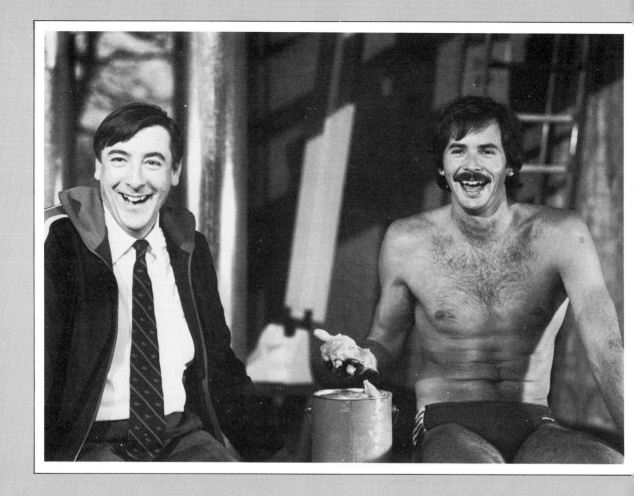

From one Channel to another
Mike Read – a profile of one of our television guests

*Mike Read was unlucky in the early part of his swimming career.
He was selected to swim in the 1960 Rome Olympics but,
only a few days before, broke his leg in a motorcycle accident.
His luck eventually changed and now he is the proud holder of the title,
King Of The Channel, having swum the English Channel twenty-three
times – a record, and four crossings more than the man whose
performance he bettered, Des Renford of Australia.
Mike, who does not train these days for the Channel between
September and March of each winter, estimates that he makes 50
strokes per minute on a Channel swim or 50,000 strokes on one crossing.
He wears a mixture of lanolin and petroleum jelly to prevent jellyfish
stings and skin chaffing, heavy rubber goggles to protect his eyes,
and carries a light flare in case he gets lost whilst swimming at night*

5 Backstroke

Floating on the Back

Backstroke has the advantage of being the only one of the four recognized strokes where the face is continuously clear of the water. This, of course, means no water in the eyes and no water in the nose and mouth. On the other hand, it has the disadvantage of being a slightly unnatural position.

The main fear at first rests with floating. The new swimmer of any age worries about his or her capacity to stand down again after floating. Many roll over with their faces going in the water. This comes about because they try to stand straight down at the completion of their float. To avoid this, the correct technique is to bend your knees up to your chest, move your chin towards your feet and then stand up. Your hands pull the water behind your hips as you stand.

Floating on your back can be achieved either with your legs together or your arms and legs apart in a star shape. Try to take in a breath before floating and let the air out slowly. The extra oxygen in the lungs will help to keep your body up in the water. When you float keep your head back resting on the water, your eyes looking at the roof of the pool or the sky. Keep your shoulders under the water, with your arms stretching out, elbows slightly bent, to balance.

Starting Off

Start with the leg action on its own. Kneel in shallow water and then push off gently so that your body is in the right position to begin with. Synchronizing the movements at this stage is not difficult. Your head should rest back on the water so that the middle of the rear part lies on the surface. Your head is a very heavy item and it is important that its weight be carried by the water and that your neck muscles be used for breathing and not for supporting your head.

When you eventually have confidence, you should be able to tilt your head slightly forward and look towards your feet. This will reduce the amount of resistance that your head creates. For a good guide to the correct head position, get a friend to watch you while you kick. If little jets of water come over the top of your head, your chin needs to be tucked in a little more. Because your head is the governing factor for a good body position, it is important that you place it correctly. It should be kept steady. Once this is achieved you are ready to start bringing in the leg action.

Backstroke Legs

The leg action comes from the hips and has an alternating up-and-down kicking movement. On the downward kick your knees bend until your feet hang diagonally down to the bottom of the pool from the knee joint, and at the end of the upward kick the leg should be straight. Keep your toes pointed and allow them just to break the surface; imagine a football being placed on the surface where your toes are: your toes should move as though you are trying to kick it about 30 centimetres in the air. It is important to keep your ankles flexible in order to achieve a whipping up-and-down movement of the feet. The toes are the only part of your legs to break the surface of the water. Try, at the end of the upward kick, to keep your knees under the surface. The kicking action should have a steady rhythm throughout.

Correct Breathing

It is very important to develop correct breathing at this stage. Introduce a regular but comfortable and natural rhythm. Do not worry too much about breathing in, but it is most important to push used air out. Purse your lips and make a puffing, explosive motion with them. You need to exhale your carbon dioxide to replenish the oxygen needed for the exercise as you go and it is therefore important to get rid of this air continuously. If the carbon dioxide is not pushed out, your legs will tire more quickly. Failure to breathe out correctly is the single most common fault amongst improvers.

Variations on the Kick

Backstroke is a swimming discipline which requires a strong kick, particularly when the stroke is swum at speed. The leg kick can be strengthened by gradually increasing the resistance and making it more difficult. Try the kick with one arm above your head. Then try putting both hands together above your head in the air. Follow this by putting both arms on the surface straight behind you. The first and third movements raise your hips but lower your feet, thereby increasing the strain. The second

movement drops your hips and your feet, doubly increasing the resistance because your arms are being held above your head.

Backstroke Arms

The general direction of the arm movements is alternating and backwards. The propulsion from the pull comes from a backward, rowing-like movement. The hands are turned out during the recovery over the water, so that the little fingers enter first, though it is also acceptable to place the back of the hand in first. Many people find that putting the little finger in first leads to early tiring because it constricts the muscles of the shoulder too much. However, of the two it is the better method because it brings the hand into the correct pulling position more easily.

Imagine your body as one large clock, with your head at 12 o'clock. Your hands enter between 1 and 2 o'clock and between 10 and 11 o'clock above your head. They are then driven back through the water into a position where your fingers are about 40 centimetres beneath the surface. Here the water is undisturbed and it is easier to get a better grip. Your hand is now slightly cupped and turned towards your feet. Your arm stays straight as your hand be-

Left: This sequence begins with my left hand about to get hold of the water to be pulled back. Note that I have lowered my left shoulder in order to get my hand in a little deeper. I then push back with my left hand to my feet. My arms resemble a windmill, my right hand entering the water as my left hand completes its pull at my thigh

gins to make the long journey towards your feet.

When your arm is level with your shoulder, your hand is then pushed directly towards your feet and in so doing, bends to 90 degrees at the elbow with the hand movement finishing under your hips.

Stroke Timing

The legs help the balance of the stroke. They are also responsible for propulsion. The most powerful rhythm is six leg kicks to every two pulls, although it is possible to swim with two, four or eight kicks. As one hand enters the water, the foot on the opposite leg should be coming towards the surface at the end of the up kick. The other foot should meanwhile be at its lowest point in the recovery before the up kick.

Right: These photographs show more clearly the rhythm of my leg kick. I make three upward kicks with each leg to every two arm pulls. Not only do the feet provide propulsion but you can see how effectively they provide balance. As my right arm enters the water, my left foot is making its upward movement, and vice versa. I try to raise my head on the surface rather than to push it back too far

Six *Splash* Checkpoints for Backstroke

1. *Fault: Water gets into my eyes and nose.*
   Correction: Look towards your feet.

2. *Fault: I have no leg power.*
   Correction: Try pointing your toes on the up kick and kick with a straight leg. Keep your knees under the surface.

3. *Fault: My face goes under the water.*
   Correction: Too much head roll – fix your eyes on a line on the pool roof. (It's better to make corrections on backstroke indoors.)

4. *Fault: My legs tire very quickly.*
   Correction: Concentrate on breathing out at least once every time your arms go round.

5. *Fault: A lot of water comes off my arms when they are recovered over the water and runs into my face.*
   Correction: Lift your little finger out first as your arms are taken out of the water and keep the arms straight.

6. *Fault: My pull takes my feet sideways.*
   Correction: When your arms are level with your shoulder in the pull, push straight towards your feet with your hand.

Gold medal Chain

Adrian Moorhouse – the second of our television guests

Eighteen-year-old Bradford grammar schoolboy Adrian Moorhouse
is very hopeful that he will follow David Wilkie and Duncan Goodhew
to breaststroke gold medal success. Adrian was ranked number three
in the world over 200 metres breaststroke in 1981, in what was
virtually his first serious international swimming season. He gets up at
5 a.m. each morning to go to the Leeds International Swimming Pool
where he trains at the Central Club under Great Britain team coach
Terry Dennison. Last winter he spent two weeks with Dennison
training in the Soviet Union. He feels that their swimmers are stronger
than ours because they devote more time to weight training.
One of the original reasons why Adrian took up swimming when
younger was that he was asthmatic. He no longer suffers from asthma

6 Breaststroke

Breaststroke is the smoothest but probably the slowest of the four recognized strokes. As a competitive swimming stroke it has been gradually refined to produce the much more rapid, revving stroke of today. The leg action very closely simulates the movements of a frog's legs and may provide most of the propulsion. It is, however, very difficult to learn and children who cannot conjure up a mental picture of the leg movements find it even harder.

Adults, on the other hand, have more rigid ankles and tend to pick up the stiff-ankled kick of breaststroke more easily.

Leg Movements

The best way to start is by concentrating on the leg action. Hold onto the pool gutter or rail. Lift your feet up off the bottom and extend your

legs behind, pressing your elbows against the pool wall for support.

Let your legs rise nearly to the top of the water by pointing your toes. Now, from the fully extended leg position, bend your knees outwards and keep your toes curled up. The heels are lifted towards your behind and the soles of your feet are then presented to the water in preparation for a backward movement. The action of your legs should be both simultaneous and symmetrical. Do not lift your knees *under* your hips as this creates resistance.

The legs now straighten with the feet moving circuitously and the toes remaining curled. The heels are brought together and, at the very last minute, the toes point to provide a little whipping movement. Bear in mind the action of a frog and you will not go far wrong. Try this movement time and again while holding onto the rail. Try to feel the water pressing on your feet as though there were real pressure against the movement. At first, it may feel as though your feet are going round and not achieving anything, but this kick is not natural to us and unfamiliar to the muscles involved. It will take time for it to become second nature.

After plenty of practice, take a float and try the kick across the pool. Your lower legs may well be down in the water. Aim to lift your heels to your behind. Drawing your knees up too far or drawing your upper legs under your body will increase drag, so keep your heels as close to the surface as you can.

It is tempting to point the toes and scissor the kick round because it is more comfortable. It may be faster in the first instance but will

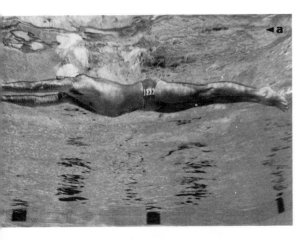

This side view of my breaststroke clearly illustrates the leg movement. The legs start straight. Then they bend at the knees so as to lift the heels. Note that my knees are not drawn up under my hips. As my feet move towards my behind, I start to curl them at the toes so that the soles of my feet are prepared for the backward press

prove slower in the long run. Try to persist with the movement which feels the most difficult. This in itself is mentally hard to do. Go slowly until you have mastered the correct movement. Unfortunately, swimmers often do not realize they are kicking incorrectly as they cannot see what they are doing. Working with a partner on the poolside who can tell you where you are going wrong is an advantage.

Correcting the Screw Kick

The most common fault in the breaststroke is the screw kick, or dropped knee. It can take a fair amount of land work to get it right. It comes about with many swimmers because of water pressure on an ankle and knee structure that is not designed to cope with the movement of lifting the heels to the behind in preparation for the kick. The water presses on the curled toes as the knees are bent. This, in turn, forces the out-turned knee back in under the body. The result is unbalanced movement. The trouble is that you cannot see the position of your legs behind you and that makes correction difficult.

Start out on the side once again. The best way of correcting such a fault is by employing the old-fashioned kick. Turn the knees out sideways and place the soles of your feet together while bending and drawing your knees up. By having your toes tucked out of the way, you can feel the position of your feet, and therefore the rest of the leg, without looking. There is no water pressing on your toes to spoil your leg alignment from this position.

When your heels reach your behind, turn your feet out and present your toes in preparation for the backward movement. Then go into the normal breaststroke kick. After a little practice, this can be tried in the water. Work at it steadily and do not hurry the movements. Working with a float can help.

For those people who find their knees are out of alignment during the kick, a rubber band, made by simply cutting a cross section of a bicycle tyre, can be used for correction. Place the band around your knees and carry out the kick with just your lower legs. This will help prevent the knees from moving into an incorrect position until the lower leg movements have been mastered. It can be practised either by holding onto the rail or with the aid of a float.

Arm Movements

The breaststroke arm action should be round and never straight backwards. Your arms start straight out in front with the palms turned outwards. The correct feel is now one of sculling out and then sculling in, or parting the water so that your head can go through it.

Your hands pull out and your arms stay straight until the hands have been pulled at least half a metre wide of the respective shoulderlines. The aim is to keep your hands about 15 centimetres under the water at this stage. From this position, the hands pull the water in a circular fashion outside the shoulderline but bend at the elbows as if to pull the water back behind your body. When your arms pull level with your shoulders, the inward scull starts and this is achieved by clapping your hands together under your chin. Your hands are then extended out in front once again.

Remember that your hands should always stay in front of your face and your elbows in front of the shoulder line. The pull should never be so big that the length of the levers reduce the application of power.

Here you can see my arms pulling wide of the shoulders before being bent in a hinge-like movement at the elbows. The hands are brought together slightly in front of my face before the arms are straightened out

Stroke Timing

The rhythm of the stroke should be: pull, breathe, kick. The movements slide over one another and you should never pull and kick at the same time, as the power of each movement would be decreased. The lifting of your head for a breath should come between halfway through the pull and the end of the pull. Prior to that, the head is down and exhalation comes in two phases. Some of your air is expelled as your arms are beginning their recovery in front of your face, and a second exhalation follows at the end of the forward movement.

Body Position

For breaststroke to propel you continuously through the water, it is vital that your body be in a completely straight line at least once in every stroke cycle. This streamlining means that the full kick is exploited before the next stroke is begun. Try never to carry your head too high like a swan, nor move it from side to side as you go. The top of your eyebrows should rest on the surface when your head is in the water.

Some Ingredients of my Stroke

Many of you will only want to swim breaststroke for fun, but those people who swim at speed might like to follow one or two of the technical refinements that I managed to incorporate in my stroke. Swimming the Wilkie way is not necessarily easy, simply because the stroke was designed to suit my body type.

I try to pull very wide. This helps to get a good feel for the pull because of my long levers – as I'm well over 6 feet tall, I am long-limbed and consequently have long muscles. When I pull in front of my face, I lift my shoulders relatively high in taking a breath. This helps to make my arm recovery looser and easier. I also try to kick into my pull and in so doing really reach forward to get good length out of the forward trajection of my whole body.

These photos show my stroke from the starting position. The arms are pulled round and wide of the shoulders. The elbows bend and the hands cut back in in front of my face. As the hands come together in front of my face, I draw up my heels ready for the kick. My feet then drive my hands on through the water. The final photograph shows my feet before completion of the movement, when my heels are together

Six *Splash* Checkpoints for Breaststroke

1. *Fault: My legs seem to drop down too far.*
   Correction: Allow your head to follow your fingers as they go forward. Drop your head a little lower into the water than before by looking at the bottom of the pool.

2. *Fault: The water goes up my nose when I breathe out.*

   Correction: Start to breathe out before your face touches the water.

3. *Fault: I do not seem to get any power from my legs.*

   Correction: Make sure that your hands are cupped up under your chin ready to be extended forward just before your heels are brought up to your behind. The forward movement of the arms should then be synchronized with the backward movement of the feet so that your hands begin their forward movement before your feet kick back.

4. *Fault: I still do not get any power from my legs.*

   Correction: Make sure that not only do your toes remain curled during the backward movement of your feet but that they also snap together at the end of the movement as your toes are slightly pointed. Imagine your feet to be rather like the end of a boat propeller: propulsion is a function of the number of different surfaces presented to the water. The more surfaces, the greater the propulsion.

5. *Fault: When I have finished pulling, I have difficulty in getting my hands back to the front.*

   Correction: Try not to make the pull quite so far back. Aim to keep your elbows in front of your shoulders during the pull, or better still, your hands in front of your face.

6. *Fault: I seem to start kicking before I have finished my pull.*

   Correction: Try to count the rhythm to yourself – pull, breathe, kick.

7 Butterfly

Like everyone else, I find this the hardest of the four strokes. I used to devote time to butterfly because it formed part of my individual medley swim. Despite the gruelling nature of the stroke, I often see recreational swimmers in public swimming pools using it. Let us then look more closely at the dolphin butterfly.

The Dolphin Kick

When learning the butterfly stroke it is best to start with the leg action. This is called the dolphin kick, as it resembles the undulating tail action of that mammal.

One of the most important things to remember when doing this kick is to keep your body relaxed and flowing. In order to imitate the dolphin movement, begin by holding your breath and swimming under the water on your front. You can either keep your arms extended or put them down by your sides. Keep your knees close together and turn your toes slightly inwards, allowing your legs to work as though one. Now kick your feet down and up, as though you were shaking them. It is necessary to keep your ankles flexible for this action. If you try to get your toes to 'whip' at the end of the down-and-up kick, this will give greater efficiency to it.

As you kick up towards the surface, your knees will flex a little and it is the force provided by the back of your legs on this movement that gives forward propulsion, along with the force on the shin and upper foot on the downward kick as your legs straighten. Your feet should only just break the surface on the upward kick, and the kick depth should be about 40 centimetres. The dolphin kick emanates from the hips through to the feet with a progressive undulation. Therefore it is important that you allow some up-and-down movement from your hips. It is as though you are shaking from your hips to your toes.

Once you have mastered this kick under the water try the same action on the surface with your face resting on the top of the water. In order to strengthen the legs and trunk movements try kicking with a float held in front of you. One of the big problems with using a float for this dolphin movement is that it tends to make the kick a lot higher than it actually is in the full stroke, when you have water on top of your behind as well as pressing on the sides.

The most beneficial kick to practise here is the fishtail kick. This is swum by holding one arm in front of you whilst resting your head on that shoulder. Keep the opposite arm down by your side. Turn your stomach to one side and kick sideways. This is the same movement as a fish makes. You can try the movement the opposite way round by looking in the same direction on the way back, which in reality means turning the body round. This kick can be executed without a float, allowing your body to be under the surface. Remember to exhale through your mouth to prevent water going in your nose and mouth.

The Arms

The arm action of the butterfly is rather like a double frontcrawl. Your hands enter the water simultaneously in line with the shoulders; make sure that your hands are in line with your wrists, facing forward. Your fingers should enter softly and not be crashed through the water surface. Then try to pull your hands together in front of your stomach and finish the movement by pressing back towards your feet. As your hands come close together in front of your stomach try to keep your elbows up as they bend. When your hands extend back towards your feet the correct feeling should be one of pushing your body out on the side of the pool.

At this stage it is best to practise the arm action with your face on the surface and holding your breath. Once you have mastered the feel of using both your arms at the same time, attempt to swim the stroke with your head pressed down even further so that the water just covers the top of your head, and keep going until you run out of breath. The main difficulty at this early stage is in getting your arms out of the water. Start by pushing off from the bottom of the pool and throwing your arms over the water. Try to shake down with your feet and to pull your arms out a second time without standing up. Each time that you push off from the bottom, try to go for a further stroke until you have managed about five strokes with your head in.

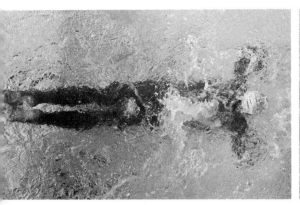
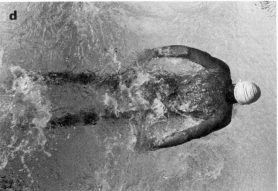

Stroke Timing

The time has now come to fit in the correct breathing. For this we have what we call the 'two head befores' rule. You want your head to go in before your arms enter, and you want your head to lift up before your arms come out. This avoids the weight of your head adding to the strain on already tired shoulder and neck muscles. By following the rule, this head weight will be borne periodically by the water.

Place your head in the water and float carefully along the surface. Bring your arms over the surface and immerse them in the water. Now pull and, when your arms reach the end of the pull, lift your head up to breathe. Your chin should go slightly forward to inhale. Do not lift your head more than 8 centimetres off the water at the chin when you take a breath, and remember to open your mouth. Your arms should now come over the water again and follow your head back into the water. As soon as your face re-enters, begin to blow as you feel your arms go in. Try to continue in this manner.

Time your leg action in relation to the arm pull as follows. As you immerse your hands, kick down (the up kick will automatically follow) and kick down again as your hands press back towards your feet. They should kick up as your head lifts to breathe. The rhythm of this movement is: kick, kick, fling. Do not kick your legs as your arms are recovering over the surface. If you find it difficult to time both the kicks, try keeping your legs still but flexible for the first kick and then just kick as you press back towards your feet with your hands. In other words, the second kick is the best one to practise first, as this levels the body in a horizontal plane and helps to push you up to breathe.

My hands enter the water as my feet kick down. As I lift my head up to breathe, my knees bend slightly and my heels are lifted back towards the surface in preparation for the knees downwards movement. As my hands re-enter the water, I kick down. Note: I do not kick as I pull

a

b

c

Six *Splash* Checkpoints for Butterfly

1. *Fault: I find it difficult to get my arms out of the water to make the recovery.*
   Correction: Try to look under your body towards your feet and so make the head lower.

2. *Fault: I still find it difficult – my hands seem to get stuck at the fingers.*
   Correction: Try to explode your air out at the end of the pull and aim to whisk your fingertips upwards before pulling your arms over the water.

3. *Fault: My arms catch the water as they come over.*
   Correction: Turn your hands to face outwards and then down just as they go back in. You may find that having your arms and hands facing down on the recovery encourages your elbows to catch the surface.

4. *Fault: My legs drop down towards the bottom.*
   Correction: This can be corrected by looking under the body towards the feet during the pull.

5. *Fault: I do not seem to get any power from the kick.*
   Correction: You are probably trying to kick during the pull. Always try to kick *either* at the start and end of the pull *or* once at the start, *or* once at the end. Try to avoid kicking and pulling at the same time.

6. *Fault: I cannot go more than about 5 metres without becoming so tired that I cannot go on.*
   Correction: Give yourself more time in practising the kick. You have probably tried to go on too fast and have not devoted enough time to some of the earlier practices.

Busy but fit!

Bill Sirs – the third of our television guests

*Sixty-two-year-old Iron and Steel Trades
Confederation secretary Bill Sirs is something of a
fitness fanatic. He runs regularly, swims
occasionally, and keeps himself in superb physical
shape. Bill swims a good front crawl and has
ensured that the whole of his family can swim. He
himself learnt in the sea when he was about five.
Bill strongly feels that more people should continue
swimming into old age*

8 Starts and Turns

This chapter considers starts and turns not only for the competitive swimmer but will, I hope, tempt recreational swimmers to use them during their fun lengths. Over the years British swimmers have often been criticized for the poor quality of their starting and turning. Certainly this is a feature of British swimming which has improved. The Americans led the world in starting and turning in the 1950s and 1960s, and still do. However, with a great number of European swimmers attending American universities, their slick techniques became adopted in Europe and the gap is now closing.

Front Crawl

The front-crawl tumble turn is one of the most enjoyable of all the turns. Once mastered it is a very efficient way of turning around in the water. Start by doing a somersault in the middle of the pool. Tuck your knees up and place your head in the water. Pull, with your hands in line with your wrists and your fingers facing down,

Freestyle: This girl freestyler shows the rotating movement of the body as it approaches the wall. The behind goes up towards the pool roof as the chin is tucked in. The feet are then projected towards the wall ready for the final push

towards your stomach and stay tucked well in. You will go round in a circle through a vertical range.

When you can manage this quickly, try the same movement in front of a pool wall. When your feet come over your head, feel for the wall with them and push off on your back. In other words, you are doing a half turn from your front to your back. At this stage it is best to start your turn about an arm's length, or slightly less, away from the wall; you should find your feet will be able to get a fix for you to push off on your back. Remember, as your feet touch the wall you should be face up.

When you have mastered this stage go on to the next. In order to judge where the wall is in relation to your turn, it can help if you start by swimming into the wall on breaststroke quite slowly. As you get about 1 metre from the wall take a breath and drop your chin down. Pull your hands in towards your stomach, as you did in the somersault, and let your feet come over your head. You may find it comfortable to start exhaling as you drop your head down, as this will prevent the water going into your nose. When your feet hit the wall turn your nose down to face the bottom of the pool and push off. As you push off from the wall, blow air out explosively as you go into the glide position with your arms extended. Do this several times

until you have mastered coming out from the wall the right way round, and then attempt to swim towards the wall using front crawl.

When you swim front crawl into the tumble turn, do not look up at the wall before you turn as this will hinder the momentum of the movement. It is best to inhale on the last arm stroke before you need to turn. The turning distance will depend on the speed at which you are swimming. The faster you swim, the further away you need to be from the wall, so it is a matter of experimenting until you find the correct distance which will enable you to get your feet to hit the wall as you turn. When you pull yourself down at the beginning of the turn you can either use both arms, or just pull on one arm and keep the other by your side.

It is important to tuck your chin in for the turn at the correct time. When you have inhaled, let your face return to the water. Then, when your recovery arm has entered and you start to pull, tuck your chin in. It is important to keep your head well in until your feet hit the wall because your body naturally follows your head.

You may well ask yourself what is the use of all this? Why not just swim up to the wall, grab the end and then push off again? Well, tumble or somersault turns are faster and have a good, bouncing feeling about them. They look more professional and, as you become more proficient, can be easier than the ordinary grab turns.

Backstroke

The backstroke turn is the most difficult of the four, because most of the turn takes place with the head facing up towards the ceiling. Let us examine the turn from its very first stages. Like the front-crawl tumble, it can be both fast and impressive and is therefore worth being able to do. Also, like the front-crawl turn, it is best to learn piecemeal in the early stages.

Go to the middle of the pool and lie on your back. (As with the backstroke itself, it is best to practise the turn indoors rather than have strong sunlight getting in your eyes.) Now bend

Backstroke: *backstroke is probably the most difficult of the turns. The sequence of movement is: hand out, head back and knees up. The palm of the hand faces up towards the roof as I drop my head back in the water. As my head goes towards the bottom, my knees lift up and my feet are placed against the wall ready for the push-off*

your knees up to your chest. With a sculling movement of the hands, turn your body through 180 degrees on the surface. The sculling movement can be achieved through practice. Keep your eyes fixed on the pool roof, circling your hands in the water with palms facing downwards.

When you can do that easily, position yourself near a wall and try the same movement in

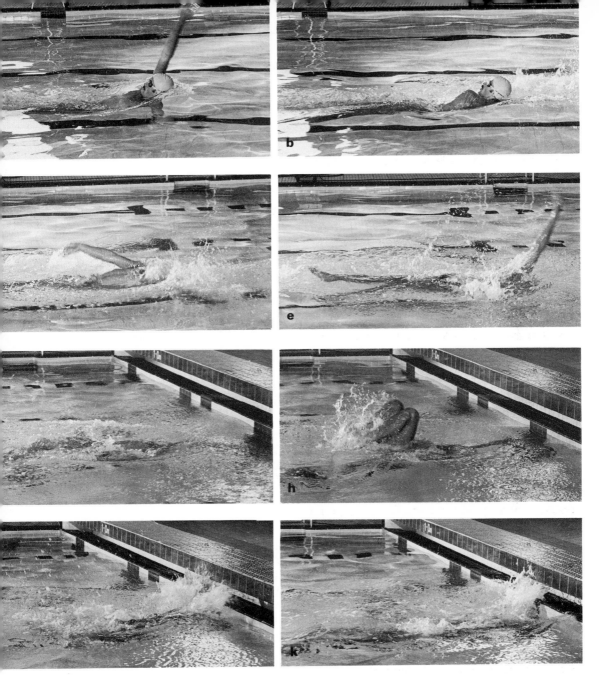

such a way that your feet land against the wall at the completion of the 180 degree turn. Follow this by reaching one hand above your head and touching the wall, palm upwards. You may need to drop your head back to make the whole movement a little easier. Once again, the knees stay bent throughout the movement. When you feel your feet touch the wall, give a light push so as to straighten your legs. The movement is almost complete; now once again swim in on your back. The order should be: hand out, head back, and, this time, place your feet where your hand was on the wall. When your feet hit the wall, draw your hands above your head and push and glide about 5 centimetres under the surface. In this last case, aim to blow out as you push. If you find that water goes up your nose, purse your lips.

Butterfly and Breaststroke

These two turns are very similar and are easy to pick up. Approach the wall on which you wish to turn by stretching and reaching out rather than shortening your stroke. You should touch the rail with two hands. Hold the rail firmly and bend your elbows so that you are, in effect, drawing yourself in towards it. Your head will now also be drawn close to the wall. Aim to bounce off the wall by taking one hand down from the rail and placing it in the water for stability. Your other arm now bends and follows your head as it moves back away from the wall. Try to look at the water after touching the wall, rather than the wall at the other end, as the latter has the effect of dropping your feet down too low for the push-off.

As your feet move up to the wall for the push-off, your head drops back under the water. A breath has been taken prior to this in order to sustain you during the push. The arms are drawn up and then straightened as you push with your feet.

On the breaststroke, it is a good idea to let your body drop slightly before the push-off; you can then extend your push-off by means of a pull under the water.

Butterfly: *the butterfly and breaststroke turns are very similar. It is important to try to make your last stroke before the wall a long one with the head down. The hands should then reach out for the wall simultaneously and slowly bend at the elbows as your head moves closer to the wall. I keep one arm in the water for balance and throw the other over the surface as I look back at the wall before my push-off*

9 Diving

There are two types of standing dive. Of the two, the racing dive is the most commonly used, frequently with a running movement on the poolside during public swimming sessions. The plain header, on the other hand, is the basic form of standing dive employed for diving competitions. It would not normally be used in a race.

The Racing Dive

You should build up towards this steadily. Sit over the edge of the pool with your feet on the scum trough or rail. Stretch your arms above your head, with the upper part of your arms close to your ears, and point your fingers in a straight line up towards the pool roof. Now push lightly with your feet, attempting to straighten your legs as you do so. Your body should now steadily uncoil as you direct your fingers towards the water. Your fingers and hands enter first, with the rest of your arms and body following in a straight line.

The direction of your body should make a flat arc under the water. Aim to get your fingers in first, so that they make a hole for the head. Take a breath before going in and blow out on entry. Now slowly lift your body up but keep to the same arc. This upward movement is associated with confidence.

Try a kneeling dive on one knee with your other leg out behind you. The arms are again stretched out above your head. Follow this with a crouching dive and then move the crouch slowly up until you are standing. You should now be ready to perform the racing dive itself.

In the correct position for the racing dive, the feet are about 8 centimetres apart. The toes are curled over the edge of the pool. Your body should be bent and your head positioned so that the eyes are focused about 2 metres in front on the surface of the water. Your arms can be held either behind your body, about half a metre behind each hip, or carried in front of

Here you can see me using the grab start, a dive used by many of the top swimmers in the world today. My feet are slightly apart and my hands are put over the edge between them. My aim is to get my hips up high, to bend my knees and then kick back so that my trajectory is deeper than in the everyday racing dive. But I do not want to go too deep; I want to try to slide under the water where there is more speed and less resistance

c

your body about half a metre in front of your head and in line with your shoulders.

If your arms are in front of your body, the first move should be to draw them back. (There is a distinct advantage here because of the shift of weight.) The arms swing back as far as they can and as they begin to return forward, squeeze the wall with your toes. A push of your feet is combined with a throwing movement of your arms, which are directed diagonally towards the bottom of the wall on the other side of the pool. By doing this, you should cut cleanly through the surface.

You should avoid slapping your forearms or chest on the surface, or, on the other hand, going too deep. The aim should be to cut the water to a depth of half a metre. By doing this,

there should be extra momentum from the glide under the water.

If you wish to start with your hands behind you, the arm movement is reversed. Your arms simply go from behind to the front position.

There are several more complicated racing dives, including the swing start, an adaptation of the track athlete's start, and the pike, which you can see me doing. My aim here is first to get my body and then my hips as high as I can before cutting into the water by piking and dipping my head. There is more momentum and more glide from such a movement; these can be increased by drawing up the heels and kicking back in midair before the pike downward commences.

The Plain Header

You do not always have to use a racing dive. If you are not going for speed and distance, then the plain header is probably the smoothest dive to use. Before learning this dive, it is a great asset to be able to perform the racing dive.

Start with your feet about 2 centimetres apart. Your body should be upright and straight. Place your arms straight above your head, fingers and hands pointing diagonally away from the shoulderline. Your body should be in a Y position, the palms of your hands facing outwards, your eyes looking forwards.

Keeping your body upright, the next movement is a bending of the knees to about 90 degrees. This is coupled with a slight flexion of the elbows, with the arms moving slowly together. Now push yourself up as though reaching for the roof. On this up jump the hips are thrown slightly forward. At this stage your eyes should still be looking forwards with your arms close to your ears. At the height of this dive, look down towards the water. As with the racing dive, your fingers enter the water first, followed by your head and then your body, but on this occasion you should aim to get your body entering the water in a perpendicular line. Point your toes on entry – this should straighten your legs. There should be as little splash as possible: you should try to get your feet to enter the same hole as your hands.

Once you have entered the water, keep your hands and arms stretched over your head, as though in a vertical glide position, until your feet have entered. This will allow your body to travel down until you can feel your feet under the surface. Now look up towards the surface, gently arch your back and swim upwards. It is important to use deep water for this dive.

Peter Squires, president of the Highgate Diving Club, which over the years has produced many internationals, seen here demonstrating the value of stretching before going into the plain header

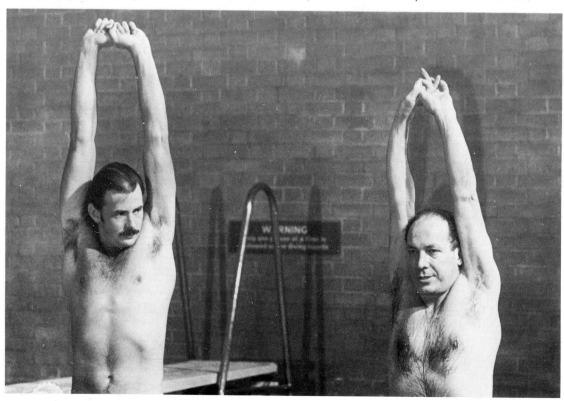

On this swallow dive from a 5 metre board, seen during the 'Splash!' television series, Peter Squires ably demonstrates many of the important aspects of diving. He gains height over the board before dropping the head and getting the hips up as the head is lowered. He finishes the dive in the stretch position with the body in a perfect vertical line from fingers to toes

10 Water Safety

The Facts

The 1980 drowning statistics, confirmed by the Royal Society for the Prevention of Accidents, make amazing reading. For instance, did you realize that over half the people who drowned in England and Wales could already swim? Seventy-five per cent of accidents occur inland whilst 25 per cent happen on the coast. Only 4 per cent of the drownings occurred in swimming pools. And 75 per cent of all victims were male.

In all there were 809 deaths by drowning in 1980. Fewer than 200 of these victims were under twenty-four years of age. Numbers in this category have continued to drop slightly, presumably because there are more and more opportunities for young people to learn to swim. Stress and depression were cited as contributory factors in 40 per cent of the accidents, whilst alcohol played a part in 20 per cent. More important, 30 per cent of accidents took place

Talking to a group of swimmers about how to conduct themselves in and around Britain's waterways. Simple instruction can start at the poolside

in hazardous locations, but warning signs were displayed at only 10 per cent of these.

What do all of these figures tell us? In the first place, too many people take too many risks. They assume that because they can swim well in a swimming pool where they can put their feet down, they are equipped for all circumstances. Many hazardous areas, particularly on private grounds, are not marked with warning signs. In addition, many are not protected adequately by fences, and access is both easy and tempting for children. Often fences these days have been vandalized. Even uncovered water butts, cattle troughs and ponds have proved dangerous.

If you are in a position to protect against these hazards, do so. Fence in home swimming pools and place warning notices. Do the same with mill lodges, urban waterways and other proven black spots. Use the National Code for Bathers.

If you are a parent, never leave young children in danger areas – always supervise them. Do not ever swim alone, particularly on an unpatrolled beach. In the sea, always try and swim parallel to the beach to avoid being sucked out into the deep by tides.

Good Manners at Swimming Pools

The Institute of Baths Management has produced a notice which is posted at most pools in the country asking bathers not to do certain things in order that all swimming-pool users can enjoy the facility. Unfortunately, the notices are often ignored simply because in some pools they appear to have become part of the furniture.

As a matter of hygiene in swimming pools, use the shower and the toilet before swimming. Do not use the pool if you have a skin infection or an uncovered infection of the feet. When in the pool, do not splash or push people. Ducking can be dangerous, as can running around the poolside and jumping in or diving on top of someone else. It is all very much a matter of common sense. Swimming underwater for long periods can lead to sudden blackouts and is therefore not recommended. Leaving your goggles on the pool deck where people can slip on them can also be dangerous. So can going into the water headfirst without putting your arms above your head. If you did this your head would have no protection, should the water be too shallow.

Some Dos and Don'ts in Open Water

One of the major concerns with both inland and coastal waters in this country is that they are generally very much colder than indoor swimming pools. The drop in temperature alone can prove quite a shock. Never go swimming in the sea when two red flags are flying on the beach. These flags spell danger. Never go swimming on your own in open water, especially if there are no lifeguards on the beach. Never go out in a boat without wearing a lifejacket. This applies whether you are a good or bad swimmer. Good swimmers are equally in danger should they knock their heads or be rendered unconscious. If you are a youngster, never play about near rivers or canals, particularly if the water is dark and of unknown depth.

If for any reason you do get stuck on your own in open water, survival is of paramount importance. You have to make assessments according to the power of your own swimming and the distance you may have to swim. If you are confident that you can make it and you are wearing shoes or an overcoat, take them off, and remove any other heavy woollen materials. Do not panic and swim off at a steady pace.

On the other hand, obvious support may not be at hand and you may have to hold out for a longer period. Try to grab hold of a piece of wood, a paddle, a plastic container, or even blow up a plastic carrier bag. These are just a few of the objects that fall into the water during boating accidents. Hang on to these objects and try to conserve energy. Heavy clothes can be shed but remember, if you are going to be in cold water for a long period, that they may

Two ways of blowing up trousers. On the left, the waisted area is squeezed with one hand, knots are tied in the legs and air is blown through the waist area. On the right, the trousers are thrown into the water and held at the waist on impact

help to conserve heat and to cushion layers of warmer air between your body and the cold water. Taking off shirts and trousers and inflating them to help you float can be easier than treading water. I would suggest that the order of priorities should be:

1. float
2. tread water
3. float with the aid of clothing.

Tread water by remaining upright in the water. The hands circle and make figure-of-eight or sculling movements in the water whilst the arms are positioned with bent elbows at either side of the hips. The feet make upright breaststroke movements. If you know that you are not going to be capable of doing this, it is a good idea to use one of the drownproofing methods of floating. I suggest that you float vertically in the water. Drop your face under the water and when you need a breath, press down with your hands and merely lift your head up above the surface to inhale.

Floating without hope in the sea can be ter-

rible and if you are anywhere near open water, it is always best to wear light-coloured clothing so that you can be seen from the air should there be an accident. If you decide to float on clothing, trousers are the easiest to inflate. Whilst treading water, tie a knot in each leg and hold the waist end of the trousers above your head. Throw the open end down towards the water and on impact grab the whole of the open end, trapping the air which enters. Alternatively you can squeeze the waist, and blow into the waist end.

Rescuing Others

The Royal Life Saving Society suggest that you *reach, throw, wade* and *tow.*

If you need to save someone in the water try to lie down and reach out for him (or her), either by hand or by throwing a piece of clothing towards the person, so you can tow him in. If the person is out of reach, throw something that he can use to help him float. In shallow water, wade to help if necessary.

Finally, if you have to go in, never approach a person bigger than yourself from the front. An hysterical, drowning person can be extremely strong. Always approach from behind and, if necessary, throw a piece of clothing towards him and use this as a means of towing him in.

On reaching land, the person you have rescued may be either unconscious or exhausted. If you get out of the water, he may slip underneath. Therefore it is best to land the victim by placing one of his hands on the other whilst you place one of your own hands on top of both. Press down with both of your hands and pull yourself out onto the side whilst maintaining firm pressure on the other person's hands.

Now crouch down yourself. You have two choices. The first is to pull the victim straight out so that his upper body rests over the top part of your leg. This is achieved by placing one foot forward and bending your knee. Once the victim's body has been brought to rest in this manner, hold his head at the back as you place his body on the ground, so as not to let the head drop.

The second method is as follows. Once on the side, crouch forward and hold your subject's right hand with your left and vice versa. Dip his body into the water twice and on the third movement pull it out and turn the arms so that the subject is now facing away from you in a sitting position. You should now both be facing the water, with the other person immediately in front of you.

The first method is obviously more useful if you are lifting out someone who is much heavier than you.

Extended Tow

There are two tows that I use when practising life-saving. If ever you are in such a situation, you might like to use them. The first is an extended tow. This would normally help in the case of an exhausted swimmer. When practising, get another swimmer to lie on his (or her) back with his arms by his side and with feet and legs together. Place a cupped hand under your partner's chin and, keeping your arm straight, turn your body on one side and swim with one arm in front, pulling in a dog-paddle manner and kicking with breaststroke legs. You should lead your partner as you tow.

This young boy is showing that it is possible to tow a passive but larger girl by using an extended tow

Chin Tow

The most useful tow for moving a panicky victim is the chin tow. Turn the subject on his back. Encourage him to keep his legs straight and his arms down by his side. Position your own body so that you too are lying on your back. Place one arm over the front of your subject with your hand firmly holding his chin. Try to ensure that you do not cover your subject's mouth or restrict the throat with your fingers, as this will hinder his breathing and cause him to panic more. Now tow him in by using a lifesaving kick (as it is commonly known) or inverted breaststroke legs.

There is obviously a great deal more to lifesaving, and I would suggest if you do develop an interest in this aspect of swimming that you read the Royal Life Saving Society Handbook thoroughly.

The hand is held steady during the chin tow in a cup position, so that the subject's head does not move from side to side

The beautiful side of swimming
Mary Stavin – the fourth of our television guests

*Mary Stavin, Miss World 1977, cannot remember when she first learnt
to swim. She thinks that it was back in her home town of Orbero, Sweden,
when she was about three years old. Now twenty-four, she tries to swim
at least once a week, to see friends, tone her muscles and keep
herself feeling fresh. She finds no evidence of chlorine-affected skin,
bedraggled hair and muscles appearing in the wrong places to put her
off swimming, and feels pretty girls look quite natural in water*

11 Additional Water Skills

There are a variety of water skills that do not fit conveniently into any category. I have put them all together here and I hope that you enjoy them.

Sculling is one that many people like to learn early on. You merely lie on your back with your arms by your side, feet and legs out straight, and your eyes directed towards the pool roof or sky. Then you make a figure-of-eight movement with your hands beside your hips. The correct movement here can be achieved by trial and error. You will know when you have it right because your body will start to move forward, albeit headfirst! You can also try lying on your back and moving feet first. Do not kick with your legs, but pull the water back behind you in a breaststroke-like movement. Races like this can be fun for the family.

The survival jump or entry is both a fun skill and useful. The aim is to jump in the water whilst keeping your head above the surface. It

Three methods of floating: (below) the mushroom float in a tucked position, (opposite) a star-shaped float on the back and a star-shaped float on the front

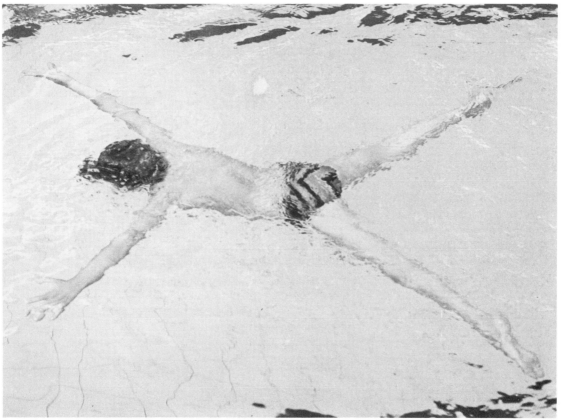

is important to enter open water in this way in cases where you cannot see under the surface. To dive in would be foolhardy. Start by standing on the deck of the swimming pool. Your feet should be together and your arms by your side. Take one step forward into the water, with your arms spread out in line with your shoulders. Lean forward with your chest, the under part of your upper arms and your legs all catching and cushioning the body in an umbrella-like effect as it enters the water. On impact, scull vigorously with your hands in order to keep the upper body high. Your face should always look to the front and never enter the water.

The surface dive is a further skill, essentially used by children. It can be employed to collect a rubber brick or other objects from the bottom of the pool, or for swimming through hoops placed on the bottom. The movement is sometimes called a duck dive, for obvious reasons. Swim breaststroke out into the middle of the pool until you are in a position where your hands are immediately above the target area. Then, instead of making a normal breaststroke pull, make a similar pull but direct your fingers at the start down towards the bottom. At the same time, drop your chin onto your chest and let your behind come to the surface. As soon as your behind bobs up, point your toes up towards the pool roof or sky and straighten your legs. You should go down towards the bottom in a straight line.

It is also possible to go down feet first. Swim breaststroke along the surface, stop, draw your knees up towards your chest and throw your hands up into the air, palms uppermost. As you throw your hands up, straighten your feet towards the bottom and then sink down. Bend your knees and squat on the bottom before travelling along it headfirst. Diving through hoops or for bricks can be a further variation.

Handstands on the bottom of shallow water are enjoyed by most children, and can be a good preliminary to the sitting dive. Please remember, though, that as soon as you put your hands on the bottom there will be greater pressure from the sides than if you were doing a

handstand on land. It can take quite a lot of practice.

Fun for the Family

Children are more likely to learn to swim if they can have fun as well, and particularly if they can attend the local swimming pool in small groups. Here are some suggestions for encouraging your children in the early stages.

For those who have just learnt to kick with a float, a kicking competition can be enjoyable. In another game, two partners face each other in the water, each partner placing his or her hands on the other's shoulders. They should then push off the bottom and start kicking against one another, the object being to push one another back with the strength of the kick.

Children also enjoy just playing tag, but the rules should preclude them from leaving the water. Other popular choices are Simon Says and What's the Time, Mr Shark? (see page 15). Both, of course, are common playground games that have been adapted for the water.

Children also love relays of all descriptions. In the early stages, walking relays across the shallow part of the pool encourage children to get used to the water. As soon as confidence on all strokes has been gained, mixing the arm and leg movements up on all four strokes can help to strengthen the swimmer. For example, mix backstroke arms and inverted breaststroke legs. At an advanced stage, a towel relay can be great fun. This is one in which the participants are asked to keep a towel dry by holding it over the water whilst swimming.

Anyone can also have fun with early diving. Picking coins and objects up from the bottom of the pool can be followed by seal dives. Lie flat on the pool deck with your head over the edge of the pool. Pull your body forward until you tip of your own accord, slowly headfirst into the water. Before entering the water, lift up your arms and point your fingers in a normal dive manner. Your arms stay above your head

Fun for the family but more serious for David Wilkie – as he prepares for another Channel 4 programme at Barnet Copthall pool

throughout the completion of the dive so as to protect the head.

Many of you will find, though, that some activities possible in the sea would not be appropriate to public pools because of the nuisance they cause. Piggybacks can cause accidents and ball games are not encouraged.

For those children who have difficulty with their breathing, blowing table-tennis balls along the surface can help, and such races can be fun. Kicking legs only or swimming full-stroke backstroke with a plastic cup on the head can encourage a youngster to keep his or her head still. Kicking with a float on the front can be made more entertaining by balancing a toy object on the float as a challenge.

12 Experimenting with the Water

If you go down to the pool on your own, use the time to find out a little more about the water and the effect it has on your body. I am going to give you one or two ideas which may set you thinking when you are practising the strokes.

Start by simply standing in the water. Put your hand in and with your palm on the water push it sideways to a position where your hand is about 5 centimetres under the surface. It should feel relatively easy. Now try it with your hand about half a metre under the water. It should be much more difficult. The reason? The water lower down is undisturbed and much more difficult to pull. It therefore follows that in that position, pulling is more effective; so, *lesson one*, on backstroke and front crawl do not be afraid to pull with the hands in a fairly deep position, as much as 45 centimetres under the surface.

Keep standing in the water. Place one hand on the surface and press down hard. It should be difficult to move your hand through the surface but easier after your hand has broken it. The movement may be accompanied by a dull thudding sound and a jet of water spurting upwards. Now try sliding your fingers through the surface and pressing down. There should be less resistance around the surface area because this time you have not caught an air pocket under your hand. Therefore, *lesson two*, always try to slide your fingers down a hole in swimming both front crawl and butterfly. Never slap, always slide, and you will get a much better grip on the early part of the movement.

There are many such tests that you can set yourself and it is certainly worth spending time experimenting with the water. A third idea is to lie flat on the water with your arms stretched out in front of you. Start with a float between your legs in order to keep them up and in a straight line with the rest of your body. Now make a breaststroke action by pulling your arms bent and back towards the shoulders. You should feel the water coming back and hitting your shoulders. Now turn your hands out and pull round and then in. The water should now feel as though it were outside your bodyline. *Lesson three*: try to keep the breaststroke arm movements wider than the shoulderline. Inside the shoulderline there would be two forces counteracting one another.

Keep the float between your legs and lie on your back. Lift both arms under the water until they are level with your shoulderline. Turn your fingers so that your palms face away from your body. Now press back with your hands and direct them towards your feet, keeping your arms straight until they reach your sides. Follow this by putting your arms up again, but this time when they get in line with your shoulders allow your elbows to bend to an angle of 90 degrees as you start to pull them down towards your feet. Towards the end of this pull, let your arms straighten as they reach your sides.

Lesson four should show that bending your elbows and pushing back in the backstroke movement is more powerful and creates less strain than trying to pull back with your arms straight.

You can try other tests which will tell you a lot about all of the isolated little skills which go together to make one swimming movement. Take a stroke that you have so far found hard; break it down into its components and go down to the pool and experiment.

13 Some Land Practices for Learners

The importance of being flexible in the water cannot be over-stressed. The body has to be sufficiently supple to imitate the movements of a fish. All the great swimmers of our time have this major asset.

I see many learners and improvers who do as many things to hold them back as to send them forward. The simple reason for this is that they cannot get their bodies into the right position in the water and this, in turn, comes about because they are not flexible enough. For those of you who know you are stiff and rather nervous in the early stages, I am going to suggest a range of easy mobility or stretching exercises that may improve your capacity to make the right type of movements in the water. You may find that five minutes spent on the poolside doing these exercises before you get in the pool helps enormously. If you are there for a lunchtime swim and find that you do not have time, I would suggest that you work on these exercises in front of a mirror at home.

Front Crawl

Let us start with the front crawl. At least once in every arm cycle, one arm is over the water, and for half the time the movement takes.

British Olympic swimming team physiotherapist Tony Power puts me through my paces. You need considerable practice to reach this stage of flexibility

Along with the difficulty of this movement, you have to remember that you are turning your head to breathe. This area must, therefore, be elastic. The first exercise, then, is to try just sitting or standing and rolling your neck in a circle on its axis. First go one way and then the other. You may find this makes you dizzy and that you therefore need to keep changing directions.

Next, lie over a bench or on a bed and imitate the alternating leg movement of the front crawl. This is quite simple but very effective. It helps to increase muscular control in the abdomen and upper leg. If you have a partner to help you on the next exercise, you might like to take turns. In the television series I used a swimming bench but at an early level a partner can be just as good. Bend over and get your partner to face you. Your partner merely holds your hands and acts as a resistance whilst you make the front-crawl underwater pulling movements.

So, in a nutshell, you have three exercises which will help your approach to the stroke. You only need devote about five minutes each day to the exercises.

Backstroke

For the backstroke, ankle mobility is a great asset. First of all, try the backstroke kick whilst lying on your back over a bench. Then follow this by draping your body half over the poolside. Support your body from behind with your hands. Now make the backstroke kick with your legs meeting the resistance of the water. Point your toes and try not to let your knees come out of the water too far.

It is also important to make sure that there is a fair degree of shoulder mobility. Keeping your arms in time with one another, swing them in an arc above your head and then back and round. Make this more difficult by using a towel. Hold the ends of the towel in front of

your stomach. Now, take it back behind your head, still gripping both ends of it. The towel should finish up across your behind.

Breaststroke

The breaststroke is very different from the other strokes in muscular terms. But again, going through the arm pull with the resistance of a partner helps rehearse the movement as well as develop the shoulder muscles.

The leg extensors are also used in breaststroke. Squatting down and then bouncing is useful. Standing on one foot and just driving the other foot, curled, towards the ground can help describe the line your legs will kick through. Another useful leg exercise is to lie flat on your face on the floor, keeping your knees on the ground, and then try to place the outside of your feet on the ground on either side of your hips in a breaststroke-like movement. I would suggest that you do not do this last exercise with a partner because there is a danger of him exerting too much pressure on the ankle and knee joints.

Butterfly

Butterfly strokes require the greatest looseness. The basic exercise is to bend forward and make the butterfly arm motion. Keep your head down and try not to allow it to be forced up when your arms circle above it. Try to keep your arms loose but feel them brushing against your ears during the circle.

Another ankle-stretching exercise equally beneficial for all strokes but particularly helpful to the butterfly, is this. Kneel on the ground with your feet flat and the soles uppermost, toes kept straight and not curled. Then merely throw your arms above your head and rock back on your feet, stretching the ankle region.

14 What to Wear and How to Wear It

Goggles

Apart from swimming costumes, goggles are the item of equipment in most common use. There are some twenty companies manufacturing goggles alone. They are extremely useful for protecting the eyes, which tend to smart in modern swimming pools, particularly in strong sunlight. Goggles, if not used properly though, can be dangerous. Always put your goggles on carefully. I would not advise holding them away from the eyes whilst the elastic is round the back of the head. The elastic structure may break or the goggles may twang back in the eyes. The result has, in some cases, been blindness. Always take the elastic side off first when removing goggles.

Some swimmers have problems with goggles slipping off and subsequently filling up with water. Try to put the eye-pieces of the goggles on first, pressing them against the bones around your eyes so that there is a fair amount of suction. Then stretch the elastic round the back of your head. Try to place the strap towards the top part of the head to provide better support. When you dive in, tuck your chin in at the last minute. This will prevent the impact of the water's surface from knocking the goggles down.

Goggles tend to mist up and the best way of demisting them is by licking the inside. Lightweight goggles left lying around can be a nuisance, as people may slip on them when walking round poolsides; so put your goggles in a safe place when you are not using them, and not on the side itself.

Swimming Costumes

This is very much the age of lightweight swimwear, both for speed and comfort. Costumes made of lycra and synthetics abound, since those made of wool or heavy materials tend to increase drag and water resistance. Some materials hold water or cling too tightly to the body, and are therefore to be avoided.

Swimming must have been hard in 1908. This typical family seen at Margate shows how cumbersome costumes were at that time (Popperfoto)

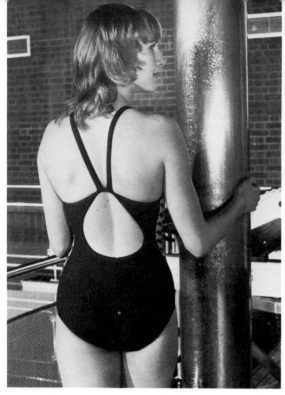

Caroline Holmyard, the European duet and team synchronized swimming champion, wearing a modern competitive costume. It is much more functional than the costume worn by Mary Stavin (see page 53). The costume provides ample support for her training routines and yet leaves the shoulders free for easy movement

Men's costumes are not designed entirely on the basis of fashion, though belts tend to increase weight; cords sewn into the costume lining are much the easiest to tighten in the water. Those men's costumes that have a skirted front also tend to increase drag. Most men's competitive swimwear can also be worn by fun swimmers these days and I would therefore suggest that anything, made in a lightweight material, that cuts away high on the legs would be good.

Women's swimwear designs change regularly. Women's swimwear has moved a long way from the time that Roman women bathed at home. Costumes in those days were often made of leather with thong-tie sides. There is an example in the British Museum.

The first reference to British women's costumes was in 1449, in Bath, when women wore smocks. Up to the turn of this century, women wore bloomers and heavy woollen fabrics. In 1909, Annette Kellerman, the Australian swimming champion, was arrested and caused a national scandal by wearing a one-layer swimming suit which covered all of her body except for her head and arms.

Things are very different now. Competitive swimmers wear costumes that are very tight-fitting and made of lycra. Fun swimmers wear bikinis or one-piece floral suits. However more women are tending to adopt the lycra skinsuits worn by competitive swimmers. It is best to wear what you know suits you and what feels most comfortable.

Manufacturers maintain that a woman's swimming costume can survive much ill-treatment and therefore should be bought to last at least one summer. Generally, though, a woman's costume suffers damage from sand, sea, salt and sun-tanning oils, and the colours are affected by direct sunlight. The materials used for lightweight costumes these days are not very durable and tend to ladder, be destroyed by abrasive surfaces, or just rot. Chlorine in water will destroy costumes and towels. To prolong life, costumes should be rinsed after use and the manufacturer's instructions for drying followed.

A woman's costume should be comfortable, allowing the legs and shoulders free movement. As a general rule, when the costume is fitted, you ought to have about 5 centimetres of lift at the top of the shoulder straps. This is very much a matter of personal preference, decided by trial and error. Competitive swimmers may find that certain styles rub the skin; this can be eased by applying petroleum jelly to both the costume and the skin in the affected area, usually around the armpits.

Prices for a standard 85 centimetre costume can vary from £5 to £14. Some styles and colours can cost up to £20.

Other Helpful Items

There are numerous other aids to help you in the early stages of swimming. Hand paddles can be obtained in many shops. These help the arm strokes and create extra resistance when the hands enter the water, thus building extra power where you need it. Flippers have much the same function in building strength in the upper legs. It is not a good idea to put children of less than four years who are learning to swim into flippers, simply because they find balance when standing in water difficult.

Armbands are standard these days at swimming pools and are recommended. They should be worn as close to the armpits as possible, though this does tend to limit movement. The air can slowly be let out of them as learning proceeds. To do this start with the chamber positioned closest on the shoulder; this will help to increase balance with the loss of support.

Unfortunately, many adults who are learning to swim have an aversion to armbands. They may feel armbands are a child's aid or draw attention to the fact that they cannot swim. If you feel armbands are not for you, kick-boards and floats are recommended. There is a complete range and most floats of the foam type, polystyrene base or inflatable kind are helpful. Always hold these floats at the side with your thumbs on top for balance.

15 Some Medical Advice

My purpose in this chapter is to give you some guidance on how to deal with certain swimmers' ailments. Most of these are straightforward and easily cured. *Injuries* in the water, despite the statistics on death by drowning, are few. Most hospitals report only the occasional case, normally caused by slipping off the poolside or diving off a board without first checking what is underneath.

Cramp

Cramp is probably the most common problem. It is brought about by chronic contraction of certain muscle fibres which 'lock', when the limbs cool after exertion. It is also caused by salt loss due to excessive sweating. If you do feel cramp coming on, keep near to the poolside where you can use muscles that are still functional to get to the edge. When the pain makes it very difficult to move a particular limb, come to the side of the pool. Do not stay in the middle, because it will not improve. A menstruating woman affected by cramp should move to an outside lane and float relaxedly.

The affected area requires heat and stretching to release the 'knot'. Most cramp occurs in the calf muscles, the toes or in the armpits. If you get cramp in your legs or toes, curl your toes back up. Sit opposite a wall and place your feet flat against it. Now just straighten your legs and bend your knees at 5-second intervals until the pain goes. Cramp in the armpits is more difficult to relieve. A warm shower may help, followed by some gentle stretching in which your elbow is lifted up towards the ceiling and the hand of your affected arm pulled down behind your head.

You risk cramp if you swim after a heavy meal, when much of the circulation is devoted to food absorption and is therefore not available to the muscles.

Stitch

Doctors are not absolutely certain what causes the sharp pain around the rib cage called stitch: it may be pressure on the diaphragm. I would suggest that if you are swimming lengths, you just ease back a little but keep swimming and exercising until the pain eases.

Earache

If you feel a sharp pain when your ear makes contact with the water, leave the pool. Do not put anything in your ear but dry the outer part of it with a clean, warm part of your towel. The towel must be clean, or using it can cause greater infection. Consult your doctor as soon as possible.

Sore Eyes

Try wearing lightweight goggles, but take care when putting them on, as the elastic strap may cause them to spring back, injuring the eyes. If you do not feel comfortable wearing goggles, I would suggest that you try washing your eyes in cold water at the end of the swim. Alternatively, bathe them in a solution of one teaspoonful of sodium bicarbonate in a bowl of warm water. Some swimmers get 'pink eye' or conjunctivitus in mild form. There are products designed to relieve this condition. Nothing cures sore eyes, though, like lying down with the eyes closed for ten or fifteen minutes.

Athlete's Foot

Fungal infection of the feet, scaling and itching between the toes is a nuisance and there are a great number of sufferers. Drying the areas between your toes after each swim will help greatly. It is important to use a clean towel. Most chemists stock preparations and powders to keep the region between your toes dry. They should be applied whenever you change your socks.

Verrucas and Warts

At the first sign of these, please consult your doctor, as he is much better qualified than anyone else to advise you. Generally, you can continue to swim if you have plantar warts, provided you cover them with a plaster.

Tendonitis

This tends to affect the competitive swimmer or length-swimming recreational swimmer. It occurs in the shoulder, and the pain is caused by continuous movement of the arms in the overarm action. It is not common among length-swimmers on breaststroke, but occurs more on the other three strokes. The tendon structure and shoulder girdle is not equipped to withstand the continuous movement and becomes inflamed. A complete rest from the stroke that you swim most of the time is recommended.

Competitive swimmers may be treated with steroid injections and instructed to rest under medical supervision; they may continue exercising the other muscle groups used in swimming. Tennis elbow caused by sculling in synchronized swimming may be treated in the same way.

Complete Breathlessness Every Time You Swim

I would recommend that you consult the swimming pool's professionally qualified coach for advice. He may suggest that you see a doctor. This condition could be caused by any number of things.

16 Swimming as Therapy

In line with our theme 'anyone can do it', one of the great aspects of swimming as a sport is that it is accessible to all sorts of people who do not normally have the opportunity for physical activity. Swimming strengthens ailing limbs, allowing full freedom of movement, because they do not have to support the weight of the body. For people with respiratory problems, the regular patterns of breathing can help the lungs. Swimming is not, however, normally recommended by doctors for those who have had heart disease.

Asthmatics

For the last two years, I have had a special interest in asthmatic children and the help swimming can give them. Swimming helps asthmatic children to lead a more normal, active life. It helps them to understand the illness, cope with the condition and overcome the fear of exercise-induced asthma. Some hospitals, for example Kings Mill Hospital, Mansfield, now provide hydrotherapy for asthmatics.

Regular swimming develops an asthmatic's toleration of both intensity and duration of exercise. Swimming groups of asthmatics also report that the activity almost never causes wheezing. Any asthmatic interested in taking up the sport as a means of combating the condition should contact the Asthma Society and Friends Of The Asthma Research Council, 12–14 Pembridge Square, London W2 4EH.

Often asthmatic children are discouraged from taking part in other sports at school. This can lead to them being over-protected at home. It is therefore advisable that if you are asthmatic you join a small group of about ten other people with the condition who want to take up the sport. Contact your local hospital's paediatric and chest clinics for details of groups in your neighbourhood.

The optimum length of a swimming session is between thirty and forty-five minutes and this should be preceded by the taking of preventive drugs five to ten minutes beforehand. Attacks can be brought on by continuous exercise over a period of between six and eight minutes. Shorter bursts of swimming are less likely to induce such attacks. The swimming session should be broken down into three parts, beginning with a warm-up lasting about ten minutes in which the swimmers are systematically introduced to higher and higher workloads. The body of the session should consist of twenty minutes of short-burst exercise. The exercise would finish with a team game or competition.

It may be difficult to assess the benefits accruing from the sport, but you could consider keeping daily records of asthma symptoms such as coughs, wheezes, shortness of breath, ability to take exercise and sleep disturbance, as well as the number of days off school and the number of admissions to hospital.

Physically Handicapped Swimmers

This is such a highly specialized field that I have to confess there are greater experts than myself; I have drawn on their knowledge and experience here. I also make a few observations from my own experience for you to consider.

Getting In and Out of the Water

These two activities may seem relatively simple to able-bodied people but of course they are very difficult for handicapped swimmers. First of all, try to find a pool with an outside ramp up to the entrance, and where it is possible to wheel a chair to the poolside. But avoid troughs of water. Many learners' pools these days have shallow steps with a rail. Swimmers who are severely handicapped and very heavy may be fortunate enough to have the use of a hoist: more and more pools are adding hoists to their range of facilities, but in addition pool attendants should be trained in handling techniques so that they may help those people who do not need to depend on a mechanical aid.

For disabled swimmers who find the steps too steep, rolling off the poolside can solve the problem of how to enter the water. It is advisable to place a mat over the edge of the pool to prevent skin burns and a helper should be in the water. You can be helped out of the water by being 'bounced' out but never let anyone pull you out by your forearms. You should be lifted from under your armpits and legs whilst in a sitting position. This does not then put a strain on any one part of the body. Pulling someone out of the water is very dangerous as helpers are likely to slip on wet steps. It is better for the helpers to lift the swimmer from a sitting position on the poolside. The ease with which this can be achieved will depend on the weight, size and degree of disability of the person concerned. In fact, for all of these suggested methods, generally speaking the handicapped swimmer will be the person best able to advise the others on how to help.

Unfortunately, the standard local authority swimming pool is not ideal for a handicapped person, but a learners' pool with a temperature of 90°F, although often too shallow for adult swimmers, or a main pool at 86°F are advantageous. The higher water temperatures allow the disabled swimmer to relax without getting too cold, and to maintain peripheral circulation for muscular activity. Let us look closer at some of the disabilities that swimming can help.

Polio

This disease damages the nervous system and consequently can lead to permanent muscular damage. Because it can result in muscular paralysis, these swimmers may lack balance. Compensatory movements in swimming strokes must therefore be made. For example, if the right-hand side of the swimmer's body has been paralysed, the movements made with the left arm and leg must be so directed as to keep the body in a straight line. Thorough drying at the end of the swim is important here because of the risk of interigo, maserated, sore skin. Cold may cause chilblains.

Spastic Paralysis

This comes about because of damage to the spinal cord or brain, often bringing about too much rigidity of the muscles. Problems with swimming will depend on the number of operable limbs. Getting the swimmer to relax in the water and to breathe out with control is important, and such confidence can only come about by feeling the upthrust of the water and by experiencing gentle movement in warm water. Learning to stand up from the horizontal floating position or reach for the poolside to rest is important, and I would advise that the method for the standing float suggested in Chapter 10 be followed.

Preventing a spastic from taking in water through the mouth or nose is particularly important because this can result in spasm. This means there must be great concentration on exhaling. Often swimming on the back is more comfortable as the mouth is then clear of the water. Too much exhortation of a spastic swimmer to try harder can be a bad thing. It can lead to already overtense muscles becoming stiffer, so that they lack the necessary looseness for swimming and its propulsive movements.

Those swimmers who are paralysed on just one side of the body may find balance and forward movement extremely difficult. The hemiplegic swimmer may find progress in a straight line even more difficult than a paraplegic. Placing the spastic arm close to the upper body whilst the other arm pulls may help prevent rolling or circling in the water. Often, though, this group of swimmers must learn by trial and error how to propel themselves.

Spina Bifida

This is a pre-birth condition which affects the spinal column and may lead to paralysis in varying degrees. Loss of sensation and incontinence are associated problems. Paralysis often occurs in the lower body beneath the site of the disease and the swimmer has therefore to rely on the muscles of the shoulders and arms to haul him through the water.

If you are helping friends suffering from spina bifida, please be careful getting them in or out of the water. They have no sensation of skin rubs caused by the body scraping the poolside.

Blindness

This of course presents special problems because the swimmer retains efficiency of movement in physical terms but has difficulty in discharging this efficiency correctly. 'Blindness' can mean anything from partial sightedness to total loss of vision. Cataracts and retinal detachment are among the many eye disorders. I know of one blind individual who swam in the River Thames quite regularly in club half-mile or mile races when over seventy years of age. Although totally blind, he was able to complete every race simply because he had a friend in the boat alongside him, with a whistle. One blow meant swim more to the left, two blows meant go to the right.

Another brave blind swimmer is Jim Muirhead. Jim has been blind since he was seventeen. He trains regularly each morning before going to work as a physiotherapist and he is the current Blind Olympic champion and world record-holder in disabled swimming. He trains length after length, counting the number of strokes each time to avoid colliding with the walls. During the television series 'Splash' we got Jim to dive from the 5 metre board, but as he pointed out, it was easier for him than we thought, because he could not see how far he had to dive!

A blind swimmer must be introduced to water gradually. He needs to be walked through much of the early stages so he can become completely adjusted to the pool and its surrounds. He will also need to know where the sides of the pool are, where the steps are positioned and the distance between his face and the water level, as well as the depth of the pool.

Breathing techniques should be learnt early so try to follow some of the advice on breathing in the earlier chapters. It is also vital for the blind swimmer to get used to having his face wet and being in or around water. When a blind person's swimming has strengthened, he will need to be helped to swim in a straight line. It is best for him to start by swimming against the side of the pool so that his arm and elbow are constantly in touch with the poolside, as a guide. Eventually, two lane ropes could be placed in one of the centre lanes of the pool for him. This should be a slightly less painful method! It is not a good idea to become too dependent on the poolside; far better to learn to swim with a helper, aiming ultimately to learn what it *feels* like to swim straight.

Other Conditions

The prevalence of various diseases and disabilities changes considerably from generation to generation. We have seen a little more of polio in the last year or so, although it was almost unheard of in the previous ten years. Thalidomide victims find swimming of great value though their condition is a relatively modern phenomenon.

Amputees find swimming a good exercise for the rest of the body. One of the main difficulties here is that the loss of a limb is in many cases fairly recent to them, and there is a resultant imbalance to be overcome by the rest of the body. Learning to experiment with head movements in particular can help amputees to achieve balance. I also talk to many people who have taken up swimming to help rheumatoid or osteo-arthritis. They find not having to carry their own body weight a great help to the affected areas. Multiple sclerosis and muscular dystrophy can also be tackled through swimming.

In general, I speak to someone at least once a week who has found that swimming helps him to do something that he was previously prevented from doing by a physical or mental condition. For these people it can provide not only valuable exercise, but a sense of achievement, gained from using a medium which calls for independent action. Swimming improves muscle tone, the cardiovascular system, balance, coordination and circulation, and provides some of these individuals with their only avenue for sporting participation.

17 A Lunchtime Swim

Many working people take a twenty-minute lunchtime swim to keep fit and for enjoyment. The swim might equally be taken after work but there are more and more lunchtime swimmers becoming involved in 'masters swimming', the aquatic version of jogging. Many adults are striving for the ASA's Adult Awards for distances covered. Husbands and wives, including many retired couples, enjoy a lunchtime swim. I want to try to give you one or two ideas as to how to get the most out of such a session.

General Training

As with any physical exercise, try to build up your training slowly. Add two or three minutes to each session. In the early stages, do not aim to do much more than ease your way up and down the pool. It is a case of mind over matter. Aim to keep going, however slowly, and try not to stand on the bottom.

After perhaps a month of this general grounding you are ready to go ahead with more specific training. Try to plan your short programme so that it is both varied and tiring. You want to be working as many different groups of muscles as possible, as well as your cardio-respiratory system.

Specific Training

Assuming that you have twenty minutes in which to do some swimming, start with a 150 or 200 metre warm-up on one stroke. Then perhaps go into 100 metres kicking and 100 metres pulling on another stroke. These items in themselves will probably take up as much as

fifteen minutes of your session. Now spend some time on repetition swims. Do, for instance, 5 × 50 metre swims on front crawl with thirty seconds' rest between each.

Test your heart rate from time to time and try to push it up, but keep it constant at the end of each swim. About 150 beats a minute would be right; the easiest way of measuring your pulse is to time your pulse for 10 seconds and to multiply the beats by 6. You won't need to take your wristwatch to the poolside: most pools are equipped with a training clock.

This is only a suggested twenty-minute session. It ought to be followed by a 200 metre loosen down on something easy like breaststroke. Gradually, on the repetition swims, you can also take your time and get a guide as to whether you are improving or not. Many swimming pools these days are setting aside lanes for adult swimming and easy lengths swimming. You will normally be expected to swim in a chain, i.e. up on one side of the lane and back on the other.

I have only covered a little of the ground on this subject. There are innumerable training sessions that you can devise for yourself, but please remember that when you go down to the pool you ought to have a session in mind and then stick to it.

Eating Habits

Many adults are interested in diets and in swimming as a means of exercise. I am often asked questions about the correct sort of food to eat either before swimming or during a swimming training period.

Swimming alone will not help you to lose weight. The only way to lose weight is by reducing your daily calorie intake. Swimming may well help you to tone your muscles. A useful way of losing weight and conditioning your muscles is to replace your lunch with a swim. Have a smaller breakfast. Do not eat before going into the water. After your training session you could probably have a sandwich and hot drink, but I would suggest that you skip heavy food.

Try to take your evening meal at about 6 or 7 o'clock in order that you have the rest of the evening to digest it before going to bed. If you are going to swim relatively hard for fitness, you should not really eat a large meal before-hand. Fatty foods take a long time for the body to break down and should be avoided. Most of these would normally be eaten at breakfast. Beer tends to lie heavily if drunk before going in the water and should be avoided. Weight can be lost by dieting but this may leave flabby skin, particularly around the stomach. Swimming is good exercise for the shoulders, arms and legs, but you will need some land exercise to tone your stomach.

18 Some Scientific Observations

Swimmers, especially adults, are frequently concerned with those aspects of swimming which contribute towards successful and easy movement. It is important to take an interest in what particular parts of a movement drive you forward, what shapes to make in the water, and why it is that some people either float or move through the water more easily than others.

For a learner and an improver, the two most important ingredients in swimming are buoyancy and ankle flexibility. Buoyancy is dependent on the downward pull on the body due to gravity (interpreted as weight) and the upthrust created by the water displaced by that body (which is proportional to volume). Archimedes was, of course, the first person to discover this relationship, in his bath.

Density is equivalent to mass per unit volume, measured in grams per cubic centimetre. The density of water is 1 gram per cubic centimetre. It therefore follows that substances less dense than water will float and those with greater density will sink. The enormous liners that put to sea float because they are less dense than water.

The density of a human body is normally about 0.98 to 0.99 and so many humans can float. The relationship between the mass and volume of humans is commonly known as the buoyancy factor. If your buoyancy factor is greater than 1 then you will sink. This happens with many adult men who just go straight down the minute they try to float. These men normally have heavier and denser bones relative to the amount of fatty tissue in their bodies. Babies are generally able to float more easily because of the amount of fatty tissue in their bodies. A person with a great amount of fat in his upper body will probably be able to float in an upright position. Your capacity to float can also be affected by the amount of air in your body. Taking in a breath before attempting to float can alter that very fine balance.

Balance

The adoption of correct poise in swimming comes about through control of balance. Most people realize that our centre of gravity is more or less where our navel is situated, but very few realize that, for some reason, our centre of buoyancy is about 5 centimetres above this. All of our swimming movements pivot around this centre of buoyancy. When we extend our limbs it slows down our rotation around that centre. When we flex our limbs it increases the speed of rotation. Drawing our limbs in towards our centre of buoyancy increases body control in water.

Resistance

The water helps to give you that 'buoyed up' feeling when swimming, but it can also make the body feel heavy. It has resistive qualities influenced by drag, surface friction and the effects of one of Newton's Laws, which states that each movement has an equal and opposite force. It is the last of these three factors that I want to look at first, because it does directly affect learners. Their natural thrashing movements are often far off course and produce reactions which do more to slow them down than the original movement did to drive them through the water.

The quickest way from A to B in a swimming pool is in a straight line. The more you deviate, the more time it takes. Almost invariably in a swimming pool the more time it takes, the more tired you become in completing the distance. If I recover my right arm over the water too wide outside my body in front crawl, that makes my hips swing to the left and my feet swing to the right and produces a roll. This is an example of 'Newton in swimming'. If I press down before pulling back on front crawl, it will have the opposite effect to the one I intended, lifting my head when I do not want it to be lifted. There are countless examples. It is therefore vital that you realize large movements too far off the centre line of your body can have a devastating effect on your progress through the water.

There is also resistance from the water to limbs or bodies entering it. This is produced by the viscosity of the water's surface as well as by air pockets trapped under the limbs before they go through the surface. In the case of your arms, getting your fingertips to enter before the rest of your hand will help.

Equally, the water will resist any movements along its surface. This is known as surface friction and is a form of drag. Drag can be the most detrimental of all of these influences. You may have seen top swimmers on television who shave all the hairs off their bodies to reduce drag. The benefits of this practice still have not been proved, but psychologically it makes these swimmers feel they are going much faster through the water. In fact, it is the advanced swimmer who is chiefly affected by body drag.

Psychological Factors

Swimming in the early stages can often be influenced by your mental approach. Feeling like a fish and not an elephant in water is going to help. Try to get the feeling of slipping through the water as though your skin were oily, like that of a fish.

Getting a Feel for the Water

This section particularly relates to the pull. Many top swimmers have what we call feel for the water. They seem to catch hold of the water and pull it quite naturally in the right direction at the right time. Although you may aim to pull right from the end of your recovery, your hands take a fraction of a second to settle in and get used to the water before making any purchase on it. This is called fixing the hands. Obviously, the shorter the distance that the hand has to move in this context, the more effective the pull. For each stroke a different shape should be made on the pull owing to the resistance of the water. In the breaststroke it is the heart shape, in the butterfly it is the keyhole, and in the front crawl and the backstroke it is the S shape.

Many adults are interested to know at exactly what point power is applied. In the breaststroke your hands describe the shape of a heart. They pull out until the water's resistance nullifies the value of the outward movement and then they pull back in under your chin. The real power of the pull comes during the second phase, after you have pulled out.

In the butterfly, your hands enter the water level with your shoulders. You then aim to pull back towards your stomach, but water resistance forces the water out wide of your shoulders. The real power of the pull comes after your hands get to your stomach. This is again during the second phase of the pull back towards your hips.

In the front crawl, the aim should be to pull back in a straight line under your body from a mid-point in front of your head. Again, water resistance means that your hands are either forced further out than originally intended, or that the pull comes even further under your body. Here the main power of the pull comes from the position just under the stomach, back towards the hips.

19 Further Goals

Having successfully conquered the early stages of swimming, you may want to go on to further goals. Let us have a look at a few of these, so that I may direct you towards the responsible authorities for further advice.

For those who are interested in personal-survival swimming (and many are!) the Amateur Swimming Association runs an awards scheme to mark achievement. The grades are bronze, silver and gold, followed by a premier award of Honours. For hardier types there is also an open-water award. Many children have the chance to enter for these awards at school swimming lessons. Further details can be obtained from Miss L. Cook, 12 Kings Avenue, Woodford Green, Essex.

If you are more interested in developing your potential for saving others, then there are many life-saving clubs throughout the country. A telephone call to your local pool will probably put you in touch with the right person. There is a tremendous range of awards for people interested not only in performing the techniques but also in teaching the subject. Further details can be obtained from the Royal Life Saving Society at Desborough House, 14 Devonshire Street, London W1N 2AT.

Adults are becoming increasingly interested in the adult award schemes and many are now practising the swimming version of jogging in an effort to achieve these awards. The one that has really captured the popular imagination has been the Supreme Award for adults for perseverance and endeavour. To achieve this the swimmer must log 1 million yards in under five years. Details can be obtained from Miss L. Cook.

Both the British Swimming Coaches Association and the Amateur Swimming Association offer awards for speed swimming, particularly directed towards young swimmers. The ASA also offers joint awards with the English Schools Swimming Association. There is now an array of awards on all strokes. It all started many years ago with the ASA Proficiency in Swimming awards, which have remained popular ever since.

If the length-by-length slog is not for you, you may wish to try synchronized swimming, the newest and most rapidly growing branch of aquatics. Often called water ballet, it can be great fun – there are even men trying it! New clubs are forming weekly and I would suggest that if you are interested in joining one of these and learning more about synchro, as it is known, you should contact the ASA Synchronized Swimming Secretary, Mrs I. Williams, at 23 Rose Hill, Bolton, Lancs., BL2 1HA.

Some of you may wish to join a diving club or a water polo club. The relevant secretaries are Mr M. Rider, 32 Norwich Road, Newton Hall Estate, Durham, in the case of water polo, and Mr J. Cook, 137 Parkway, Welwyn Garden City, Herts., AL8 6BH, in the case of diving.

More and more adults are becoming interested in long-distance swimming. It is not necessary either to be fast or to have any previous knowledge of this branch of the sport to take part. If you want to find out more about the programme contact Mr A. Humphries, 40 Brook Drive, Great Sankey, near Warrington, Cheshire. You don't have to be wealthy to go in for long-distance swimming: some people may be under the impression that it is costly because of the need to hire navigational boats.

There are many associated activities which are hazardous if you can't swim: angling, rowing, sailing, scuba diving, surfing, wind-surfing and water skiing are just a few of the sports that come to mind. Further details on these sports can be obtained from the Sports Council at 70 Brompton Road, London SW3 1EX.

20 Have We Always Swum This Way?

The four recognized swimming strokes have not always looked the way they do today. In fact, a hundred years ago, swimming was literally restricted to breaststroke.

The front crawl started as sidestroke, which was a type of breaststroke swum with the head turned to one side and with a form of scissor kick. It then speeded up and became known as the English overarm or 'side overarm'. These were developments from the breaststroke and were, of course, swum with the arms coming over the water. By moving from the prone to the side position the swimmer could lift one arm out and increase the speed of the action. At the same time, the prone frog kick eventually became a scissor-like movement as the arms were lifted out alternately.

In 1873 there was great surprise when John Trudgeon raced this way in London. The stroke became known as the Trudgeon and today can still be seen in pools being used by many of our senior citizens who have seen the stroke used by their parents.

The up-and-down movements of the modern leg kick did not develop until Dick and Arthur Cavill, two of a family of six swimming brothers from Australia, pioneered this technique just before the turn of the century. Front crawl is now swum with six leg kicks to each arm cycle, or every two pulls.

The breaststroke was the first of the four strokes to be developed and was initially always swum with the arms under the water. If you study the pictures of my own breaststroke you will notice that we now pull our arms first before lifting our head. This sequence was not really employed until 1961. Prior to that, breaststroke had always been executed with the swimmer pulling and breathing at the same time – in fact, much slower.

There were many variations on this type of stroke. In the 1930s, swimmers started to lift their arms over the water because there was nothing in race rules to prevent it. Between the mid-thirties and fifties, the Japanese started to experiment by swimming large distances underwater because this was faster than swimming on the surface. The rules changed and in 1952 breaststroke and butterfly were recognized as two separate strokes.

Butterfly is probably the most fish-like, or at least dolphin-like, of the strokes, but strangely, it is also the most recent technique. It had, as I mentioned, started as part-breaststroke, but this stroke, with butterfly arms and breaststroke legs, can be very tiring. Experiments at the University of Iowa in 1935 to test the flowing up-and-down movement proved successful because it was more natural and less exhausting. The larger muscles of the back can be used more readily than with breaststroke legs.

However, the new combination remained illegal in competition until 1952, when the butterfly and breaststrokes were divided. The first really outstanding exponent of the new butterfly dolphin, as it was called, was the 1956 Olympic champion, Bill Yorzck. Now, butterfly is some 9 seconds faster than breaststroke in world record terms over 100 metres.

The backstroke, which first appeared as an Olympic event in 1908, started life as a double-arm pull with inverted breaststroke legs. Then swimmers started to experiment with alternating arms. As soon as the front crawl became popular, they began to realize that up-and-down leg movements would be quicker and easier.

By the 1912 Olympics, the 'Old English backstroke' was becoming extinct and did, in fact, die quickly. Throughout the 1930s backstroke was swum with a straight arm pull and recovery but in a much shallower range than today. The 1950s saw this rowing-boat approach fade as a bent arm pull was introduced to develop greater power. The arm now stays straight during the first part of the pull but bends as the arm gets level with the shoulder. The elbow then bends to an angle of 90 degrees. The head is also now carried further forward in the water.

21 The Future of Swimming

Swimming is changing rapidly. The average age-group swimming competition in America is now electronically timed and the results computerized. On the competitive front, we have come a long way in recent years. In 1904 Emil Rausch of Germany was the last person to win an Olympic gold medal swimming sidestroke. He won the 880 yards and the mile. That situation would be inconceivable today. Just twenty years ago, the Royal Life Saving Society recommended approaches and tows for rescuing drowning people that were not particularly practical for anyone who was small in stature. Now the techniques are more realistic. Twenty years ago there was no such thing as personal-survival swimming. Synchronized swimming only existed in an embryonic, non-competitive form. All branches of the sport are now expanding.

There is an almost insatiable demand for leisure swimming. The concept of a 25 metre swimming pool with a parallel diving and learners' pool, favoured by most local authorities building pools in the 1970s, is still very much in evidence. But some local authorities are now building larger leisure pools including wave-making machines and separate learners' pools. There are superb examples at Swindon and Swansea.

Alan Hime: A Pool Manager's View

I won my first major games medal in 1970 in Edinburgh at the Commonwealth Games. Like me, Barnet Copthall Baths manager Alan Hime won the bronze medal in the 200 metres breaststroke, though some twenty-six years before I did. Alan went on to coach many international swimmers, including two world record-holders. He says, 'I think that swimming facilities in Britain are more and more used in the right way, thanks to more sensible structuring. Here at Copthall we are fortunate in having three pools – one for swimming, one for diving, and one training pool. This, of course, makes programming much easier. Pool managers these days have to recognize that when the weather is bad, as it has been this winter, people will not just come out to swim on their own. They have to be tempted, and we achieve this by offering them a wide range of classes, setting down lanes for what we call aquatic "jogging", and having a very comprehensive competitive programme. Having the diving pool helps to decrease accidents which come about through swimmers moving under diving boards. Again, though, good programming is the key. Our pools are never left idle during the main part of the day.'

I think there is going to be an even greater increase in the number of disabled and handicapped swimmers, but it looks as though for the average child there is going to be less opportunity to learn to swim. The economic climate over the last two years has led to tremendous cuts in school swimming. This directly affects the child who comes from a disadvantaged background. The middle-class child will still have the necessary opportunity, because his or her parents will be able to afford the more costly local authority-sponsored swimming lessons. This is one of the most worrying aspects of our swimming future, and it may be reflected in the drowning statistics in ten years' time.

On the competitive side there have been calls for a national supremo for the sport, a National Coaching Director, who would be responsible for guiding international and national swimming, and, more important, for the preparation of our teams for the major championships. Our previous national coaches have found this work to be a drain on their professional time as club coaches.

World swimming records are levelling off. A number of records, including my own 200 metres record, have lasted for more than six years – something which has not occurred on such a scale since the 1950s. We appear to be approaching the limits of individual achievement with sophisticated modern training and the intervention of science. The time has probably come for greater technical innovation. The last real major change that occurred came in the breaststroke over twenty years ago. Such innovation would produce a further surge in swimming performances throughout the world.

Of the aquatic disciplines, water polo has experienced the greatest difficulty. Lack of publicity and money, along with numerous changes in the rules sanctioned internationally, have not helped. Our poor international results have been caused by lack of training opportunity for our teams over a lengthy period. Water polo is a great sport but its future in terms of British participation at international level looks in jeopardy. Britain needs even more young players entering the game.

British diving continues to do reasonably well, though diving is very competitive. There are still no full-time professional coaches in Britain and we lack the facilities of the American universities and Russian 'centres of excellence'. On the other hand, there is plenty of opportunity these days for our competitive swimmers. Full-time professional coaches have replaced part-time instructors in many pools, and many swimmers can now train up to four hours a day. There is no comparison between the opportunities now and those available just ten years ago, and I think that this has been reflected in our results over the last decade.

Equally, more swimming pools in this country are opening for longer periods. Many open early in the morning for recreational swimmers, and there is more opportunity for leisure swimmers. With the exception of Caithness and Sutherland in the Highlands, which have one pool each, there are numerous pools in each county so most people can find one within easy reach.

Swimming as a sport now needs something new and exciting to give it that injection of public interest so necessary to all sports. Perhaps a new swimming stroke might achieve this: after all, it is thirty years since the last one was introduced. Does anyone have any bright ideas?

On a more contentious note, I think that the time has come for a reappraisal of swimming as a spectator sport. Competitive swimming needs to go open. Only that way will it keep the big star names and the colour. Personally, I would love to be able to compete still, but I am prevented from doing so as I am classified as a professional swimmer.

The time has come to create trust funds for swimmers in the same way as for athletes. Very few swimmers can actually make money out of racing, which is how professionalism is defined. Gone are the days when a senior swimmer could afford to take part without regard to his future financial security. Success requires effort and time. Is it so great a crime to be paid for doing something one is good at? Until this hurdle is overcome, swimming will remain a sport in which, in front of television cameras and the rest of the mass media, unknown youngsters compete shrouded in caps and goggles.

Swimalong with Wilkie

You may have heard of one of these events being mounted in your locality. 'Swimalong with Wilkie' is a programme of sponsored swims in which all the participants have their photograph taken with myself and receive this on a scroll of honour. I normally also give a swimming exhibition. The response to these events since their introduction in 1978 has been tremendous. We have had as many as 1200 swimmers at some of them and it has been a great pleasure both meeting so many people and being involved with so many different causes.

A happy swimming club seen at Buckie in the Grampians demonstrates that people of all ages like both swimming and swimalongs

The Royal National Life Boat Institution, Sports Aid Foundation, the Amateur Swimming Association, and the Scottish Amateur Swimming Association are just a few of the bodies with which the events have been associated, although they are carried out for a full range of worthwhile causes. The events remain as popular as ever and our current aim is to raise £100,000 towards a new lifeboat for the RNLI. In addition, nearly £15,000 needed for the preparation of the Scottish swimming team to attend this year's Commonwealth Games was raised through a Scottish National Swimalong. A sum of £30,000 had previously been raised for the preparation of our last Olympic swimming team. These are three worthwhile causes with which I have been proud to be associated.